Is This The One?

Other Books by Stephen Arterburn

Every Man's Battle

Every Man's Challenge

Every Man's Marriage

Every Woman's Battle

Every Woman's Marriage

Every Young Man's Battle

Every Young Woman's Battle

Preparing Your Daughter for Every Woman's Battle

Preparing Your Son for Every Man's Battle

Is This The One?

Insightful Dates for Finding the Love of Your Life

STEPHEN ARTERBURN

ZONDERVAN.com/
AUTHORTRACKER
follow your favorite authors

ZONDERVAN

Is This The One?
Copyright © 2012 by Stephen Arterburn

This title is also available as a Zondervan ebook. Visit www.zondervan.com/ebooks.

This title is also available in a Zondervan audio edition. Visit www.zondervan.fm.

Requests for information should be addressed to:
Zondervan, *Grand Rapids, Michigan* 49530

Library of Congress Cataloging-in-Publication Data

Arterburn, Stephen, 1953-
    Is this the one? : dating to decide if this is the one / Stephen Arterburn.
      p. cm.
     ISBN 978-0-310-33571-9 (softcover)
  1. Dating (Social customs) 2. Dating (Social customs)—Religious
aspects—Christianity. 3. Marriage—Religious aspects—Christianity. 4. Mate
selection—Religious aspects—Christianity. I. Title.
HQ801.A788 2011
241'.6765—dc22   2011008897

Cover design: Extra Credit Projects
Interior design: Beth Shagene

Printed in the United States of America

12 13 14 15 16 17 /DCI/ 21 20 19 18 17 16 15 14 13 12 11 10 9 8 7 6 5 4 3 2 1

Contents

Dating to Beat the Odds

What would you do in these situations?

Situation 1: A friend clues you about an investment deal that could double your money in only six months. With that kind of return you could pay off some bills, get the iPad you've been craving, and treat someone you want to impress to a great night out. Then you read the teeny-tiny print on the contract. It warns that there's a 50% chance you will lose your entire investment. Would you put your life savings into a deal like that?

I don't know about you, but I would think twice before going "all in" on a deal like that. It could be the same as shredding my money or throwing it away on lottery tickets. At this stage in my life the risk of loss is way too great for my blood.

Situation 2: You arrive at the airport to learn the flight you're scheduled to board has a "mechanical problem." The airline assures you it's not a big deal. There's a solid 65 – 90% probability your flight will reach its destination safely. Would you get on that plane?

Are you kidding me? If you don't rebook your reservation

on the spot and walk away from that flight, you also must love Russian roulette. I'm sure not going to roll the dice with my life by getting on that beater of a jet.

Situation 3: You hear the wedding march starting inside the church. In just a few seconds you will walk to the altar and say "I do" to the love of your life. But as the doors open and the music swells, a strange thought goes through your head, something you heard once: *For every ten couples that make a marriage commitment at the altar, one to four of them eventually un-make that commitment in a divorce court.* Are you still willing to take the plunge?

If you think this risk is acceptable, welcome to the club. Every week around the world thousands upon thousands of people who would never take risks caricaturized by the first two scenarios take the same risk (about a 65 – 90% success rate) to say "I do" in hopes of achieving a happy, lifelong, divorce-proof marriage. Actually, the risk of divorce in marriage is not as great as has been commonly and mistakenly believed. The word on the street is that half of all marriages end in divorce — a 50% failure rate. That urban myth, which has sparked great fear of marriage commitment, was the result of some shoddy arithmetic and even worse analysis. The real range of the divorce rate is somewhere between recent polls by Harris Interactive (12%) and George Barna (35%).

Whatever the actual percentage, it is still too high. It's not that we aren't trying to keep marriages together. Yet the best efforts of those who specialize in fixing marriages — therapists, counselors, authors, speakers, church leaders — haven't made much of a dent in the divorce rate for decades. And for all the excellent resources available for saving and enriching marriages — books and video programs, sermons and seminars, classes, conferences, and campaigns — the chances of avoiding divorce are not getting better.

"But, Steve, those odds don't apply to me," you may argue. "I'm a really good and loyal person and I go to church. So when I get married, I will stay married. Divorce isn't in my vocabulary."

I hear this all the time. I agree with you. It sounds reasonable that moral or church-going people should have an advantage for lifelong, healthy, happy marriages. Great idea, but it doesn't pan out in reality. The data shows the marriages of religious and even Christian people fail at the same rate as the general marriage population.

What about marriages that are brain dead and on a ventilator but never end in divorce? The statistics don't tell us about the numbers of discontented couples who stay married instead of filing for divorce. These people are married and miserable. Yet they remain married for the sake of the kids or for the financial advantages or simply because they think it's wrong to break a marriage commitment. In many cases the families of married-and-miserable couples experience just as much devastation and pain as divorced families.

There's an old proverb that says, "Marriage with peace is this world's paradise," and I believe it. I also believe great marriages require hard work. In fact, a marriage license could be viewed as a "work permit." What's more (and if you're looking for the message of this book in a nutshell, you've found it): ***Marriages that last are, in great part, the product of better decision-making before couples say "I do."*** Without this crucial front-end investment in dating and courtship, a marriage runs the risk of living out the second half of that old proverb: "Marriage with strife is this world's purgatory."

I wrote this book to show you how to beat the odds in your own journey toward a rich, fulfilling, lifelong marriage. But don't get me wrong; I'm not suggesting that dating is all about finding a mate. I really hope your life is more than just a quest to get married. Dating is something you do to have fun, to get to know people, and to learn how to have fun and get to know people. Do it with that kind of attitude and along the way you just might find a great potential partner.

So whether you're dating seriously, dating casually, or not dating at all, as a single person, your odds for a great marriage are way greater than the divorce rate. Why? *Because you're still single!* You're still on the dating side, where great marriages begin. You're not mired in a miserable marriage that defies fixing. And you're not floundering in a flood of regrets over a decision you wish you had never made.

There's an old aviation principle that applies to dating and marriage. In light of the dangers of weather and mechanical malfunction, it is far better to be on the ground wishing you were in the air than to be in the air wishing you were on the ground. As an unmarried person, you are still safely "on the ground." This is the time to decide whether or not the situation you are in, the person you love, and the timing of it all will create a great marriage.

Your desire for a great marriage must not start at the altar. It has to start right now, during your dating years. Now is when you will set a course either for a great marriage or for the misery and despair of divorce. In that sense, every dating book you read is an anti-divorce manual. Some of them are good, some not so good. I'm confident if you implement the dating concepts you read about in this book, it will make a significant, positive difference when you marry.

How can this book help? By showing you how to date creatively and wisely, have huge amounts of fun when you date, and make a completely informed decision when you do choose someone to marry. One part of this process is what I call the Ten – Date Challenge. Accepting the Challenge will equip you for a rich, enjoyable (and just plain fun) dating experience. And the Challenge will greatly increase your chance of choosing someone to marry who will help you enjoy the marriage of your dreams instead of creating a marriage nightmare.

Divorce is one of the most painful human experiences for anyone involved, and the pain seems like it will last forever. You don't want to go through a divorce to validate how torturously painful it is.

This book is about the right ways to find the love of your life and to stay happily married and divorce-free "till death do us part." But it's also about how to have a lot of fun along the way, experiencing someone you care about in some very unique dating situations. Before you say "I do," I am hoping you will say "I will" a few times to yourself.

"I will take my time."

"I will read this book."

"I will do what the book suggests before I say, 'I do.'"

So, if you are willing, read on and let the good times roll!

1

Date Wisely, Marry Well!

Life has many blessings, but few of them are as fun and challenging and wonderful as having a daughter who exceeds all expectations. This is true of my blessing, Madeline Victoria. (I'll put her up against your kids any day, even if you don't have any yet!)

When Madeline stepped into her teen years, I was one very proud dad. My cute little girl was morphing into a beautiful young woman right before my eyes. Apparently, I wasn't the only guy who noticed the transformation. She began saying things like, "Daddy, there's a boy at school who wants to take me on a date." And, "Daddy, when can I start dating?" Like a lot of protective dads, I quietly hoped I could stall her interest in boys for a little while — like into her twenties or thirties! Actually, I wasn't that paranoid, but I was in pain over the prospect of my baby girl being on a real live date once she turned sixteen.

"D-Day" — if you will — came for Madeline a lot sooner than I was ready for it. I squirmed a little inside every time a guy showed up to take her out. I was convinced no boy on God's green earth was good enough for my sweet girl. I wished

I could invisibly accompany Madeline on her dates so I could nail any gorilla-armed guy who laid a hand on her. But I was, at the same time, happy to be launching my wonderful girl into a fun and potentially rewarding time of her life.

As it turned out, I got through Madeline's early dating years just fine. But in her later teens, when the same guy kept showing up three or four dates in a row, I really started getting nervous. And when words like "going steady" or "my boyfriend" or "kinda serious" popped up in our talks, my anxiety-o-meter started cranking up toward panic. It was all coming into focus for me. At some point Madeline's dating would end, and one of her young men — maybe one I had already met — would become her husband. *Was she ready to make that choice?* When I first started thinking about it, it gave me the willies. Now, she's such a mature young woman with the kind of character I never had when I was her age. I believe with a little help from Dad she will make a wise choice.

But my greatest fear in those early days of my daughter dating was that Madeline would marry a real jerk — someone who used her, abused her, broke her heart, or crushed her spirit. And I dreaded the possibility that she would end up the victim of a devastating divorce. I wasn't about to let that happen on my watch. I wanted to do what I could to protect her from the devastating divorce process too many go through.

My fears grew out of personal experience, not as someone who counsels hundreds of men and women torn apart by divorce, but as someone who has been there. In my late forties, around the time Madeline began thinking about junior high boys (she's now in her twenties), my own storybook marriage ended in a betrayal I never suspected and a terribly painful divorce I never thought would happen to me. I was determined to do anything I could to prevent that from happening to my daughter.

And since you're likely in the same situation as Madeline (not married and dating), I have similar feelings about you. Many of your peers are married or thinking about marriage, but you're single. Maybe you're madly in love and wondering if this wonderful person in your life is "the one." Or perhaps you're still hoping and praying to meet the love of your life. Wherever you are in the wide world of searching and dating and waiting, I'm writing this book for you. Despite the tragedy of divorce experienced by so many couples, you have every reason to anticipate an awesome marriage with a wonderful partner, a marriage that will last a lifetime.

Let me tell you why I'm so hopeful for my daughter and for you.

■ A Strategy for Dating Wisely and Marrying Well

Several months ago it was plain to see Madeline and her boyfriend were getting serious. They stopped dating other people and spent more and more time together. They were beginning to talk about long-term plans for their life together.

My daughter is a young adult, so I have no legal right to tell her whom or when to marry, and I don't intend to. But I love her deeply and want the very best for her. So seeing the glimmer of marriage in her eyes, I issued a dating challenge to Madeline and her boyfriend. I knew my plan would give them the maximum opportunity to avoid the regrets and "if only's" that can lead to divorce.

I am issuing the same challenge to you. I call it the Ten – Date Challenge, and it's a big part of *Is This The One?* Now, if the idea of a challenge turns you off, please know this book is about much more than accepting a challenge. It's about changing the way you think about dating. And it's about changing what you do on dates by trying some of the fun dating ideas in these pages even if you don't want to get involved in the Challenge.

However, if you do accept my challenge, I am confident it will work for you as it is working for my daughter. Why am I so confident? Because a similar challenge worked for me following my divorce. Here's the story.

After about six months of big-time pain and isolation, I was finally able to get my chin off the floor and sense hope that life was worth living. I knew I wanted to marry again at some point and possibly have more children. But the thought of getting back into the dating scene left me cold. Having already been rejected and betrayed by more than one woman, I cringed at the prospect of revisiting those feelings with every date that didn't work out. All I wanted to do was to meet Ms. Right quickly, settle down, and leave the single life and all its drama behind. That's not what happened, but I sure wanted it to be that way, just like thousands of other singles I have met over the years.

As the host of *New Life Live*, a daily radio call-in program, I am privileged to work alongside two of the wisest men I know — Henry Cloud and John Townsend. But I don't just work with them; I seek their advice and allow them to speak truth into my life. I have never once regretted going to Henry and John with my struggles and needs.

Having walked with me through my divorce and being aware of my aversion to dating, Henry and John said, "Steve, if you really want to marry again, you have to get out there and meet some eligible women." Then they laid down a challenge and called for my commitment to follow through on it: "We're asking you to date at least twenty different women before you narrow your focus to just one."

It was a staggering thought, like being challenged to climb Mt. Everest. Twenty women meant twenty possible rejections, and the very idea made me cringe. But I trusted Henry and John's wisdom, so I agreed to follow through. (Well, I kind of agreed. Some of those dates were actually just conversations with women I met at Starbucks, but I counted them as dates because I have had dates where there was no conversation at all.)

My quest got off to a shaky start. Date Number One accused me of being "emotionally unavailable." *Ouch!* There I was, starting out on a very scary journey, and there she was representing her entire gender. Couldn't she be nice to me for just 30 minutes? The ridicule and rejection threw me back into a loser mentally. It was only one date, but I was ready to quit. Henry and John wouldn't let me off the hook.

After I got over Date Number One (and it wasn't easy), some fun and amusing dates followed. When I told a very wonderful woman she was Date Number Thirteen, she replied that since she was the horrific number thirteen it probably wouldn't go well for her. She was right, so we made a quick date. Another amazing woman I dated was one I had almost married twenty years earlier. It seemed as if we were meant to be but we parted after dating, convinced we still weren't right for each other. (If

I had not agreed to the Twenty-Date Challenge I most likely would've married her and missed the incredible life and wife I have now.)

I completed my dates with twenty different women over a period of two years. The twenty dates ranged from sipping coffee at Starbucks to a dress-up night at the opera. It was a difficult process because I had been out of the dating scene for more than twenty years. But I was committed and I persevered. And the process was rewarding because it led me to Misty, the woman I eventually married.

Henry and John continued to hold me accountable during my courtship with Misty. They coached me through getting to know my new love deeply and preparing for our life together. It was a long, thorough process, but I'm so glad my friends held my feet to the fire. Today I cannot put into words the absolute joy Misty has brought to my life, including the thrill of bringing a new son and daughter into the world together. I not only have a wonderful wife with whom I am raising a combined total of five kids, but I am free of the "if only's" and "what if's" that haunt so many who marry without truly knowing their partners or others that might have ended up being partners. I am quite secure in knowing I made a magnificent choice. And the last time I talked to Misty about it, she said she made a good choice too!

I want this same joy and fulfillment in marriage for Madeline and my other children. That's why I challenged Madeline and her boyfriend to accept my Ten-Date Challenge and begin their serious quest for the marriage of a lifetime. Here's how it works.

■ The Dating Challenge in Three Phases

PHASE ONE — *Take-a-Break Dates*

My first challenge to Madeline and her boyfriend was to take a break (taking a break is not the same as breaking up) from seeing each other and date at least ten other people. (I told them they were lucky because Henry and John made me date twenty different women!) I didn't ask them to break up, just to take a break for the purpose of gaining clearer perspective on each other and where they were headed together. It was a tough thing to ask and even tougher to do, but they worked through the request and accepted my challenge.

Your own quest for the marriage of your dreams begins the same way. Whether you're in a serious dating relationship with one special person, in a casual dating relationship with several people, or not dating at all, I challenge you to take a break. Get out there, meet a bunch of new people, and date at least ten of them. If you're already dating someone, each of you could date at least five people, so there would be a total of ten outside dates between the two of you.

There are many reasons to take the Take-a-Break Challenge, and I will give you more as you read, but here are a few for now:

Reason #1. If this is the only person you've ever dated and you want to avoid the regret of never having been on a date with someone else.

Reason #2. If you have been dating each other so long, the break would make sure you're not just so used to each other that you're mindlessly moving toward marriage.

Reason #3. If you have some doubts that need to be cleared up before you can move forward.

Reason #4. If a parent hands you the book and requires you to do it to obtain the "parental blessing" and all of the benefits that come with it.

Reason #5. If you meet someone that just might be more right for you and this is a safe, non-confrontational way to take a break and take the date without deception.

Reason #6. If you feel so confident in your future partner you want to take the Challenge to prove it is as strong as you believe.

Reason #7. If you are going to be geographically distant and you want the freedom to at least get coffee or go to a movie with someone else during the separation. Remember, it is not breaking up; it is simply taking a break.

"But," you say, "I don't even know where to start with this taking a break thing." No worries. Part One of this book has everything you need to successfully complete Phase One of the Ten-Date Challenge, including how to meet and connect with new people, fun ideas for Take-a-Break Dates on any budget, and tips for making the most of the time you spend with each new person.

PHASE TWO—Agenda Dates and Holiday Dates

If my daughter and her boyfriend made it through Take-a-Break Dating and still wanted to be together, I was okay with that. But at that point I would ask them to step up to the second stage of the Dating Challenge. I had two major ground rules for this stage.

First, I wanted them to continue dating for a minimum — and I'm talking a *bare* minimum — of one year before they got serious about becoming engaged. If you get only one concept out of this book that you totally commit yourself to live out, here's the one worth the full retail price and a whole lot more: ***Before you say "I do" and take that first bite of wedding cake, you must without exception date that person for at least one year.*** A year-long commitment to purposeful dating allows all the aspects of each person's character and personality — including quirks, habits, traits, tics, and flaws — to be experienced and known by the other. A commitment to date through the happenings and holidays of all four seasons ensures nobody will be rushing you or pressuring you to marry too quickly. Yes, I've heard of couples who dated for only two hours (okay, maybe two weeks or two months) and were happily married for eighty years. But such marriages are very rare exceptions to the rule — rarer than tidy hogs. So say it with me this time: ***Before I say "I do" and take my first bite of wedding cake, I will without exception date that person for a least one year.***

Second, in addition to anything else they did together during this time, I wanted my daughter and her boyfriend to include two specific kinds of dates. I would ask them to go on ten dates that have specific built-in agendas or assignments. The purpose of Agenda Dates is to help them get to know each other in different settings. For example, one devious Agenda Date I had in store for them was to spend a day or an evening together doing something that one of them enjoys and the other one hates. They would never come up with a date like this on their own.

But this Agenda Date was going to provide great insight into their levels of tolerance and patience with each other.

I also wanted them to go on ten creative holi-dates over their year-long journey toward possible engagement. Holiday Dates (Holi-Dates) are simply dates relating to the big holidays we celebrate through the four seasons of the year, such as Valentine's Day, Memorial Day, Thanksgiving, Christmas, New Year's Eve, and others. I wanted them to experience before marriage the relational dynamics and pressures that often surround the holidays, things that can drive a wedge between a husband and wife.

If you and your special one still want to be together after Take-a-Break Dating, I challenge you to work through ten Agenda Dates and ten Holi-Dates over a period of at least one year. It's the best way I know for you to broaden and deepen your knowledge of each other and eliminate many of the regrets and unpleasant surprises that can destroy a marriage. I've got your back at this stage too. Part Two in this book contains creative dating and discussion ideas to help you get inside each other's head and heart as you continue your quest toward the marriage you desire.

PHASE THREE — *Premarital Counseling Dates*

If Madeline and her boyfriend completed Phase Two and were more committed to each other than when they started, I would offer them my approval and blessing for engagement and eventual marriage. But there was one more stage in the Challenge I wanted them to complete. I wanted them to go on ten Premarital Counseling Dates together that centered on ten vital mar-

Date Wisely, Marry Well!

riage topics. Each date required them to meet together alone and answer some heart-searching questions on one of the topics. Then they had to discuss that topic further with a trained premarital counselor. The process would continue until all ten topics were covered.

Okay, I realize that at this point in your dating life the need for premarital counseling may seem as remote to you as "a galaxy far, far away." But the third phase of the Dating Challenge is just as important to your success in marriage as the first two. So it's never too early to acquaint yourself with the steps that loom on the horizon.

As you and the person you've chosen fall more deeply in love during your year of Agenda and Holiday Dating, engagement becomes more of a certainty. Once the question is popped and the engagement ring is purchased, you enter the final phase of the Challenge. Part Three of this book is waiting to take you the rest of the way to your wedding day and beyond. These chapters will prepare you for ten Premarital Counseling Dates with a qualified marriage counselor. The only thing left for you is to tie the knot (and keep it tied)!

10 Great Reasons to Accept the Ten-Date Challenge

Not convinced that the Challenge is for you? Waiting for me to say something like, "But wait, there's more!" to sweeten the deal? Okay, here are ten great dealmakers to consider:

1. *It's going to be fun.* You have an exciting adventure waiting for you in the Challenge. Think of how much fun

23

it will be to discover if the person you're dating really is the love of your life. And if you're not dating now, you're going to enjoy going out with lots of new, interesting, and sometimes unusual and amusing people.

2. *Leave dull dating behind.* Are you in a dating rut, same-old-same-old every weekend? Get ready to bust out of your dull routine in a big way with some great new people and some cool new ways to have fun together.

3. *You'll get valuable input.* You're going to learn so much about the person you're with through these stages of dating. And you'll find the answers to some big, big questions, such as how fast and how far you should move toward marriage in your dating relationship.

4. *It's a handy excuse.* Are you a little iffy about getting serious with the person you're dating? Does the idea of moving toward engagement give you the shakes? The Challenge gives you a valid excuse for stepping back, taking a break, and meeting new people.

5. *You'll get out of the zone.* The different people you meet and different things you do on your dates will push you and your date out of your comfort zones. Yes, this really is a benefit!

6. *It's time to face the music.* The Ten-Date Challenge gently nudges you to address critical relationship issues that the normal dating routine allows you to avoid. You'll get into discussions that will stretch you, improve your overall relational skills, and better prepare you for marriage.

7. *You'll have nowhere to hide.* When you follow through with the dating plan, there will be no more rocks for you

to crawl under. Your significant other will see you as you really are, and you will see your significant other as he or she really is. And believe me, that's a good thing.

8. *Getting to an altar-ed state.* If you and the one you love complete the Ten-Date Challenge and meet at the altar some day, you will be light-years ahead of most couples in your preparation for marriage because of how well you know each other.

9. *Staying out of court.* Great news! In my experience counseling couples for a couple of decades, the divorce risk plummets for couples who date wisely and marry well. On *New Life Live*, when someone calls with a horrible marriage problem we always ask how long they dated, and invariably it was much less than a year and the caller barely knew the bride or groom. By getting to know each other deeply, you eliminate tons of potential regrets. Divorce won't be necessary because you and your partner know who you're marrying and what you want out of marriage. You will also avoid a potentially miserable marriage marked by emotional disconnect, violence and abuse, addiction, or infidelity.

10. *Going the distance.* Huge bottom line: The Ten-Date Challenge prepares you well for a strong, peace-filled, rewarding, and enjoyable marriage that will last your lifetime.

What a promising payoff for simply investing yourself in meeting and getting to know some new people!

You may be interested to know what my daughter Madeline has gained from the dating challenge I laid out for her. As I write this, she and her boyfriend are in the process of working through the three sets of ten dates in Phase One and Two of the Challenge. Over dinner not too long ago Madeline told me about a plan she's mapping out for her life. She intends things to happen in this order: finish college, take time off to travel, get settled in a job, buy a good car, and perhaps get married at around age twenty-six. I think the Ten-Date Challenge has helped her formulate her long-term plan and make it as meaningful to her as possible. I couldn't be happier about her prospects for a happy, fulfilling life.

What about you? How do you feel about this dating concept? Are you excited or a little anxious? Are you confident about getting started or uncertain that you can pull it off? Maybe you are willing but the person you're dating is not and says "I never will be." If that's the case, this dating concept is already working for you, because this person's reticence may get much worse in marriage.

No matter how you feel right now, please work through those feelings and take the Challenge even if you have to go it alone. Now is the time to rouse yourself from your dreams of marriage and start taking the simple, solid, safe steps that will actually help get you there. The Ten-Date Challenge awaits you. Go for it!

TAKE-A-BREAK DATES

Ramping Up to Take a Break

What are you doing for the next thirty to sixty days? Slaving away to pay the bills? Playing cards with your friends as your only social interaction? Reading and writing and cramming for grades or promotions? Hanging with friends? All of the above? None of the above? Just holding on as life flies by?

Well, what if there were something you could do in the next thirty to sixty days — along with anything else you've got going — that would make your next thirty to sixty years (that's right, I said *years*) the best they could possibly be? And what if this "something" was actually a lot of fun to do?

Impossible? Too good to be true?

No, it's *totally possible and totally true!* I'm inviting you to invest a couple of months in something that will pay huge dividends for a lifetime. Who wouldn't take a deal like that! I'm talking about accepting the first phase of the Ten-Date Challenge. Take a break from whomever you're dating now (or if you're not dating at all, take a break from that) in order to meet and date ten new people. I call it Take-a-Break Dating.

Let me be real clear: I'm not saying that you should "break

up" with someone in order to date others; I'm saying take a short break from dating this person. Don't even think about making a decision about whom or when you will marry until you date at least ten other people. Ten dates before you say "I do" is a big, forward step in the direction of a marriage that will last, (or discovering that it probably won't). And, like I said earlier, Take-a-Break Dating is just good, satisfying, life-expanding fun.

In this chapter and the next, I want to give you the straight skinny about Take-a-Break Dating. Let's start with the things you need to know before you launch into your first Take-a-Break Dating adventure.

■ Take-a-Break Dating 101

When I launched into the series of Take-a-Break Dates that eventually led me to Misty, I was apprehensive about what I was getting into. You may feel the same. But once I got into it I was fine and actually had a lot of fun. You will too if you keep the following points in mind.

Take-a-Break Dates are not meant to be a big deal. Relax. You don't have to get the car waxed or buy a new outfit for every Take-a-Break Date (unless you really want to, of course). These dates don't have to be expensive, dress-up deals, even though there's nothing wrong with formal and fancy. Take-a-Break Dates can be very basic. They're just two people getting together to get acquainted. Depending on your schedules and preferences, a date can range from an hour sipping lattes together to a walk in the park to an afternoon of bird-watching (okay, maybe it's pushing it to say that is fun for most people) to an evening at the symphony. They can be as brief, simple, and inexpensive as you want them to be. And you can probably finish your ten break dates in a month or two.

Take-a-Break Dates are not cuddly romantic encounters. If you think this is all about steaming up the windows with a series of new people, you've got the wrong idea. Think platonic. These dates are meant to be one-time get-togethers with ten different people for non-romantic face time in a pleasant setting. No pressure to "be together," no lofty expectations, no strings attached. And no going to places where strings so easily get attached, like a bedroom or any place where horizontal is the most comfortable.

Now, it's very possible that one or more of your dates may cause you to feel all warm and tingly inside. That's what happened to me when I met Misty, and she eventually became my wife. I'm simply advising you to keep those feelings on the back burner (or maybe the fridge is better!) for a while. Continue through your ten platonic dates before you think about going out with any of them a second time.

Remember: You're on a mission. Your Take-a-Break Date mission is to meet and date a lot of new people in order to evaluate your relationship with any other people you may already be dating. For example, let's say you've been casually dating the same person for a while. He/she is a nice person and you like him/her, but you're not sure about moving the relationship to the next level. Take a break to expand your horizons and see who else is out there. You may meet someone new you *would* like to know much better. Or after dating several people you may realize what a good thing you have in the person you're dating now.

If you're not dating at all but would like to start, Take-a-Break Dating (minus the need to actually take a break) is the thing for you. Don't wait until you think you've met Mr. or Ms. Right. Just start dating different people and you will get a better idea who may be right for you.

Maybe you've been dating the same person for several weeks or months and wonder if this is "the one." A great way to help you make that decision is by taking time out to date others. Say something to him or her like this: "We've been having a great time, and I like you a lot. But I think it will be healthy for us to evaluate where our relationship is going. Let's commit to dating other people for a while and then talk about it. We can even tell these people that we are taking a short break from dating each other." Take-a-Break Dating will help you gain clearer perspective on your main squeeze.

Or perhaps you've been seriously dating the same person for a long time and find yourself on the verge of engagement. Take a break and date others before you pop the question (or answer it). This is especially important if you feel the least bit uneasy or unsure about taking the serious step of engagement. Use Take-a-Break Dating as an excuse to seriously evaluate whether or not you're ready to marry this person. You can even blame it on me. Say, "I've been reading this really great book that encourages couples to take a break and date others. I think it's a good idea. Why don't we do what the book recommends and see what happens?"

Keep your dating goal in mind. Since the purpose of Take-a-Break Dating is to get to know other people, your goal for every date should be to learn as much about each person as you can and allow them to learn something about you. This means the best settings for Take-a-Break Dates are those that provide plenty of opportunity for interaction.

The way we learn about people is through observation, conversation, and intuition. Through observation you notice a person's appearance, behavior, reactions, posture, mannerisms, and so on. Is this person well-dressed and groomed or sloppy? Courteous or crude? Nervous and fidgety or calm and cool? Detached or "in-the-moment"?

You also learn a lot about people through the questions and answers of a good conversation. It doesn't take long for someone's values, opinions, priorities, biases, interests, and peeves to pop up as you talk together. And it's not only what people say (or don't say) in conversation that is revealing but how they say it. Are they open, engaging, and interested in you, or are they guarded, withdrawn, conceited, and self-absorbed? Do they dominate a conversation or draw you in with questions?

And you can pick up a lot about people intuitively. How do you feel being around them: relaxed and comfortable or wary and guarded? Feelings may not be the primary gauge of a relationship, but it is wise to be sensitive to both the positive and negative vibes you get when you're with new people.

Practically speaking, getting to know someone through observation, conversation, and intuition requires "face time," so that's your goal in a Take-a-Break Date. If you get together with someone for a spectator event such as a movie, concert, or play, make sure you plan additional time before or after to sit face-to-face over a meal, coffee, or dessert for conversation.

■ The Endless Possibilities for Take-a-Break Dates

In order to get acquainted with someone, you really don't need more than a place-to-meet room and a couple of folding chairs — and you can probably get by without the chairs. But a pleasant location and a stimulating activity can sure add a lot of enjoyment to the process. So I recommend that you be thoughtful and creative about planning Take-a-Break Dates that are fun and interesting. You may already have a ton of ideas for where to go and what to do, but here are several more you may want to try out or adapt to your own style.

Coffee, tea, or pasta carbonara? Meeting over a slice of pizza or a slice of pie, eggs Benedict or Egg McMuffins, steaks or burgers, or just a hot cup of java or chai tea makes for a great Take-a-Break Date. It can be simple, sumptuous, or anything in between. Breakfast, brunch, lunch, snack, dinner, dessert — whatever you like. When, where, and what you eat is only the backdrop. It's all about sitting down face to face while the serving staff does the brewing, cooking, serving, and cleanup so you can focus on learning about each other.

Off your seat and move your feet. You may find that doing something active during a first meeting is more comfortable for you and your date than being confined to a table for an hour or more. The important thing is not letting the activity substitute pleasant conversation. So have fun getting acquainted while biking, hiking, jogging, rock climbing, kite flying, bowling, or playing golf or tennis. Too strenuous for you? Take it down a notch with activities such as mini-golf, ping pong, or a stroll through the park, the zoo, the aquarium, or an art gallery.

Take it all in. Spectator events are terrific opportunities for

Take-a-Break Dates. Who wouldn't welcome an invitation to a movie, a concert, or a sporting event that everyone's raving about? Just make sure it's an event your date will enjoy. I mean, it's okay if you like Trekkie conventions or rare insect museums or cage fighting or sitar concerts. But not everyone gets the same buzz you do from these events. Play it safe by inviting your date to join you at more widely appreciated movies, concerts, live theater, operas, sporting events, lectures, poetry readings, and so on.

A successful Take-a-Break Date doesn't hinge on how much time or money you invest. It's all about getting to know another person and allowing him or her to get to know you. Whether you walk away saying to yourself: "Thanks but no thanks." Or: "I may want to do this again." Either way, the encounter has moved you closer to the person you eventually decide to marry.

While taking the break, look for interesting people and interesting things to do. Have fun, let yourself be known, and get to know the other person. And use the time to connect in difficult situations. Rather than rejecting someone you know is not your type or going to be in your future, challenge yourself to connect with them and have the goal of helping the other person feel better about herself or himself than before the date. No matter what else you do, at least practice kindness and understanding. If nothing else, you will grow in your tolerance and appreciation for others.

■ You Have to Find Them If You Want to Date Them

When I started to date, twenty people seemed like quite a lot of folks. But it really wasn't. First of all, I was a talk show host, and as a result I know a lot of people and a lot of people know me. But my dates came from women I had been friends with while married and wanted to get to know better. Others came from those who knew me and suggested someone for me to meet. These were the ones that produced the biggest disasters. I came to understand that people really did not know what I was like or what I would like.

WIDEN YOUR HORIZONS

Ten Ways to Meet New People

1. *Get buff.* Join a gym or health club. Someone you work out with may "work out" as a great date.

2. *Get some class.* Take that class you've always wanted to take: pottery, photography, basket weaving, creative writing, stained glass art, painting, brain surgery, martial arts, wind surfing, foreign language, bonsai gardens, etc.

3. *Join a new Bible study group.* Just as long as they study the same Bible.

4. *Work the network.* Throw a party for a few single friends and ask them to bring one or two of their single friends.

5. *Book a date.* What do you like to read — I mean beside the TV schedule? Join a book club in your area based on reading interests: history, poetry, mysteries, spy novels, whodunits, bestselling novels, etc.

Where can you find people you may want to date? Start with those you already know — people who haven't been on your radar as potential dates but now could be. Remember: You're not looking for perfection, just a few new people to meet, spend a couple hours with, and learn something about. Look with new eyes at singles of the opposite sex who work with you or around you, attend classes with you, live in the same apartment building

6. *Dance with a new partner.* Kick up your heels at a dance club or class. Swing, Latin, jitterbug, hip hop — whatever gets your feet moving. You might find a dance partner you would enjoy as a dating partner.

7. *Walk or run for a charity — and a new friend.* Sign up and walk it out for charity. People who care to help others might care to meet you.

8. *Get chatty.* Log on to reputable singles chat rooms — and actually chat with people.

9. *Play ball, sport.* Sign up to play a coed team sport sponsored by the local parks association: softball, volleyball, basketball, tennis, paddle ball, lacrosse, etc.

10. *Profit from nonprofits.* Get into volunteering for nonprofits and service organizations. These people are already into connecting with others.

or neighborhood, attend your church, or who you see frequently at the gym, in your club or service organization, where you volunteer, and so on.

Next, find ways to meet people outside the familiar areas where you live, work, study, or play. When you break out of your comfort zone and try new activities you'll end up meeting new people. Don't just do something different to find potential dates; try things you might enjoy because you'll meet people who have similar interests.

Another way to meet new people is to purposely change some of your life patterns in ways that expose you to new groups of people. If you're used to leaving work and going

MIX IT UP
Ten Ways to Change Your Life Patterns

1. *Friend online friends.* Continually seek and add new online friends.
2. *Hobby horse.* Take up a new hobby and join a club based on that hobby.
3. *Change churches.* Or Bible study groups or Christian singles groups.
4. *Spread yourself around.* Start patronizing a different grocery store, mall, post office, restaurant, 7-Eleven, etc.
5. *Get a move on.* Consider finding a different apartment in a new part of town.

straight home, stop doing that. Go where people are, look them in the eye, and talk to them, rather than maintain a reclusive after-work life. If you're used to going to the same old place with the same old people, quit that too. Try some new places to eat, drink, shop, and play. New, different, challenging, and connected are the new words in your new life pattern vocabulary.

You may be wondering, "What about all the online dating services I hear about? Are these good places to meet people for Take-a-Break Dating?" Sure they are, with one major provision. If you want to succeed in finding a great person through a service you have to treat the service (and connecting to others on it) as if it were a part-time job. Your profile and pictures need

6. *Try a brand new brand.* Stop at a different coffee shop on your way to work or school.

7. *Bunch up for lunch.* Find a new place to spend your lunch hour or a different bunch of people to each lunch with.

8. *Timing is everything.* Change your workout time or routine at the gym.

9. *Get some culture.* Visit art galleries or museums you normally don't visit.

10. *Recalculating.* Take different driving or walking routes to work, school, church, the market, etc., and see who you run into.

feedback from your friends. Returning contacts and pursuing others needs to become part of your new routine. The harder you work, the more satisfying the result.

■ Once You Find Them, You Need to Connect with Them

Finding new people is one thing. Connecting with them and exploring Take-a-Break Dating possibilities is something else. By "connecting" I mean introducing yourself in a positive and engaging way. How do you make good connections with some of the new people you find as you open up to new relationships?

You'll never connect with anybody by osmosis — simply by being in the same room, attending the same class, or sitting at the same table. That's like expecting to get light out of a lamp that isn't even plugged into the wall. You need to enter that person's space, let them know who you are, and ask about them.

You need to assume that making a connection is up to you. True, occasionally someone new will step up, break the ice, and make an introduction. But if you sit around waiting for others to make the first move you'll soon find cobwebs under your arms. If you want things to happen, be ready to take the first steps.

Here are ten proven steps to help you take the initiative in making connections with new people:

1. *Look good.* Always go into group settings dressed appropriately for the occasion and well-groomed, as if you were planning to meet a date. It will help you feel good about yourself and more confident about meeting others.

2. *Say hi.* Say hello to everyone you come into contact with. You're not invisible, so don't act like you are. And when you say hello to people, smile and make eye contact.

3. *Focus on all new people.* Greet both men and women, since those of your gender may later introduce you to their friends of the opposite sex.

4. *Offer your name.* When you get a positive response to your greeting, introduce yourself by name and offer your hand.

5. *Speak up.* Make a comment about something you have in common, such as the event, activity, or interest that has brought you together. For example: "This has been a great meeting!" or "I'm kind of new here, but I'm enjoying myself."

6. *Ask polite questions.* If the person responds in a positive way, ask a question or two related to whatever you have in common. For example: "May I ask how long you've been involved in this group?"

7. *Stay tuned in.* Actively listen to responses by maintaining eye contact, smiling, and nodding or using other body language to demonstrate your interest.

8. *Dig deeper in conversation.* Ask follow-up questions based on the person's response to your first question. For example, a follow-up to the previously suggested question might be: "What other groups like this have you been involved with?"

9. *Don't hog the spotlight.* Allow opportunity for the person to ask you a question or two, but then give a brief response and turn the discussion back to them.

10. *Be cool no matter what.* Always be courteous toward those who do not respond to your greetings, comments, or questions. Your positive response may later prompt them to open up to you.

As you approach people with openness and a positive vibe, some will warm up to you and others just won't get it. Those who return your interest and positive approach are excellent possibilities for Take-a-Break Dating.

So what happens next? In the next chapter, I want to help you transition from meeting, greeting, and connecting with new people to exploring the possibilities for Take-a-Break Dating.

3

How to Make Your Own Breaks

I have to tell you right up front that this chapter may not be for you. Why? Because everything in here is stuff that most people already know. It's basic information about getting into the dating scene, tips you may have mastered years ago. But I have to include it for the few readers who really need it. These singles have spent way more time in front of a computer than connecting with other human beings. And there are others who have been in total hibernation socially for many moons but are now ready to wake up and meet some new people. If you're in one of these categories, this chapter is for you. But if you don't really need a refresher course in Dating for Dummies, feel free to skim the highlights in this chapter or skip to chapter four and save yourself some time.

Okay, if you're still with me it means you're open and ready to explore Take-a-Break Dating as a means of expanding your social horizon. That's great! Since you have a positive outlook about meeting and dating new people, you will probably find more people than you ever imagined who would love to spend time with you. But you'll have to break out of your current dating pattern — or non-dating pattern — to connect with these new people, especially if you're currently dating someone exclusively.

A lot of people resist Take-a-Break Dating because their whole life is absorbed in the person they are presently dating. They don't talk much to other people or socialize with others if their significant other is not around. Their steady is usually quite pleased and secure in such an arrangement. But how will either of them know for sure what they've got if they don't meet and date others for comparison?

This is a big problem. Not dating others or not allowing a partner to date others might reflect insecurity on the part of one or both partners. In the beginning, it is not easy to set the other person free. But in reality, when a couple is strong and secure enough to date others, it will serve them well in the future. For example, Lindsay and Evan have been dating each other for more than a year. But Evan doesn't mind Lindsay going out with another guy if he's busy. It works because both Lindsay and Evan understand that, once they are married (which they hope to be some day), the time for getting to know and enjoy people of the opposite sex in a casual-dating kind of way is over. Casual dating outside their own relationship is no big deal for Lindsay and Evan because they love and trust each other. Their marriage will be all the stronger for having tested their commitment by dating others, or not! It could lead to the end of a relationship that would end anyway one day in the future, only with much more difficulty and pain. That's the mission of Take-a-Break Dating; you either make it through or you break up because of what is revealed in the Challenge.

Lindsay and Evan understand that one of their casual dates

with someone else may turn out to be deeper than just a "nice time." If that happens for either of them, it will tell them something about their relationship to each other. It will show them that they have been less than truthful about how much they mean to each other. Hopefully, it will cause them to halt their forward march toward marriage and rethink what their relationship really means. And if they eventually break up, the Take-a-Break Date mission is accomplished again. Taking a break on a casual level works to reveal hidden flaws or weaknesses in the relationship, and it is exponentially more important to expose these lurking problems before marriage than after.

If you begin the Take-a-Break Dating journey and welcome my advice to meet and connect with new people, a few of them will catch your eye with their physical appearance, personality, friendliness, wit, or charm, and you will want to spend more time with them. (Remember, I'm not talking about having sex, just getting to know them better!) Now what? How do you move from making a connection to spending time together and getting better acquainted? Here are several things to keep in mind.

■ Don't Just Stand There, Ask Someone Out

Back in the days of people like George Washington, Clara Barton, Thomas Edison, and probably even your parents and grandparents, it was considered the gentleman's responsibility to do the asking, driving, and paying on a date. (I mean, who knows how many weekends Betsy Ross sat home alone sewing flags because guys in her town didn't ask her out.) Now, there's nothing wrong with the tradition of the guy taking the lead, of course, but it's just that: a tradition, not a rule, law, or one of the Ten Commandments. These days it is quite acceptable for either the man or the woman to say, "Would you like to grab a cup of coffee with me?" or "Want to catch a movie together sometime?" And if you get the answer you're hoping for, it's okay for either person to say, "How about Tuesday?" (That's right, concrete thinkers; Fridays and Saturdays are not your only options for dates!)

And it's totally okay for guys or girls to say, "It's my treat." Or you can just see how the date goes and when it's time to pay, if you did the asking, you do the paying. If a guy protests the idea of a gal financing the date and demands to pay, she should consider herself lucky. She can compromise by offering to pay her part, but if he still won't give up the check, it's okay for her to graciously accept his generosity. At the same time, she could try to figure out why he has such a hard time allowing someone to do something nice for him. It may be that the situation makes him feel out of control or controlled or defensive because he doesn't know how to respond to genuine caring and generosity.

When it comes to going out on a date, there are three kinds of people: those who make things happen, those who wait for things to happen, and those who have no clue about what's happening. Your only guarantee for getting a date with those who catch your attention is to be someone who makes things happen. Here are ten action items to help you make Take-a-Break Dating happen in your life.

1. *Make short list.* As you meet and connect with people, keep a mental or written list of those you want to get to

know better. When you're ready to make a move, decide which person on the list you want to ask first and what that person might enjoy doing with you on a date. That's all the list can do for you, so get off your big couch and get busy.

2. *Don't pull a Cyrano de Bergerac.* You remember the big-nosed guy from literature that convinced a friend to woo his beloved Roxane for him. Don't be like him. Step up to the plate and ask the person out yourself instead of coaxing or bribing someone else to do it for you. After all, your friend may move in and steal your thunder ... and your date!

3. *Be cool.* Be confident and relaxed. After all, you have already made a positive connection with this person in some way — friendly greetings, a few casual conversations, seeing each other in a group of friends, etc. Perhaps your morale is already high because the word on the grapevine is that this person has been asking about you. Why shouldn't you expect this connection to remain positive?

4. *Get to the point.* Having a conversation that leads to a date isn't going to happen through mental telepathy. And practicing in front of the mirror won't cut it either. You actually have to form the words and ask the person out in space and time. Ask however you can ask them — in person or by telephone, voicemail, text, or email. Just ask. The more you put it off, the more fun you're missing.

5. *Now's the time.* When asking someone out, choose the right time and place. This is a casual request for a casual date, so you don't have to be totally alone together.

47

Just make sure that the person you're talking to is not preoccupied with others when you ask.

6. *Be clear.* Here are a few examples of how to ask a person out on a break date without appearing to "come on" to him or her:

   - *"I'm going to see the exhibition at the gallery Wednesday evening. Would you like to go with me?"*
   - *"How about meeting me for lunch before class on Friday?"*
   - *"Any chance you would like to take a hike or bike ride on Sunday?"*
   - *"How about going for coffee after our group Bible study?"*

7. *Don't pressure.* Make it a winsome invitation. Don't exert pressure or lay on guilt to get a yes. And whatever you do, don't use the phrases that convey in any language that you're desperate. (Phrases like: "Pretty please," "I'm begging you," or "I won't take no for an answer.")

8. *Prepare for instant follow-up.* If the other person agrees to the date, have a plan in mind. Be ready to suggest the day, time, place, and other details. Or you may want to ask if there's a different activity, place, or day the other person would prefer.

9. *No is no problem.* If the person you ask says, "No thanks," to your invitation, don't crumble in despair or storm off in anger. It's not the end of the world. Stay cool, friendly, and polite. It will show the person that you're still interested in continuing friendship, even though a date may not happen. Wrap up the conversation with something like, "Okay, no points off for trying." Let the "no" help you start developing a more realistic relationship with that person,

perhaps a relationship that won't include even a casual date.

10. *Remember that maybe only means maybe.* If the person says, "Some other time," just say, "Sure, no problem." Then in a week or two give it another try. But if you get a "no" or another "not now," proceed with caution. You don't want to make a pest of yourself or start looking like a stalker.

It is not easy for most people to approach the first person. It is a big risk that I had to process before getting a big no. And I did get them. But they were not about me. The other person had their own agenda, own struggles, and I did not have to take every rejection personally, which is exactly what I did in the beginning. If you don't succeed with the first person you ask, don't sweat it and don't give up. Go back to your short list and ask the next person in line. There's still a lot of fun and enjoyment out there waiting for you. But of course it comes with the high price of taking a risk.

▰ Be Real, but Be the Best Real You Can Be

All right, you have a casual date coming up this weekend and you want it to be just right for this person. You want to make a positive impression whether or not it's the only time you go out together. So let me coach you in two important areas for being the best date you can be: how you look and how you act.

Appearance is important

In order to make your first dating impression positive and lasting, let me remind you about ten no-brainer areas for personal care you just cannot overlook. Yes, this is pretty basic stuff, but it never hurts to review and be reminded of some things that cannot be overlooked. The first five appearance tips on the list below you can take care of in time for a date this weekend. Tips six to ten may require an investment of time that will pay great dividends in how you look in the future.

1. *Be squeaky clean.* The old proverb says that cleanliness is next to godliness, and unless you're going out with a zookeeper who loves the pungent smell of dirty animals, you won't get close to anyone for long without cleanliness. Shower or bathe before your date. And, as your mom used to say, pay special attention to your ears, hands, and nails.

2. *Be a fragrant encounter.* You know those people you can identify by their aftershave or perfume long before they enter the room? Don't be one of them. Sure, you want to smell good, but most people are turned off by too much of a good thing. And you don't want your date to break out in a flaming rash in the middle of dinner because your fragrance incites an allergic reaction. And if you're still using the same "foo-foo water" you used in high school, consider making a change.

3. *Don't overlook whiskers and zits.* Guys, keep the facial hair shaved or neatly trimmed. Girls, put in the time to pluck or wax away unsightly facial fuzz, and use only enough makeup to highlight your natural beauty. If you battle ongoing acne or other skin problems you must cover with makeup, see your doctor about effective permanent treatment. And remember; the more at ease you are with your skin problem, the less of an issue it will be for others around you.

4. *Wear well.* Grubbies are fine for cleaning house and shooting hoops. But when you go out, make sure your clothes and shoes are clean, in good repair, and appropriate for the occasion. (That's right, cutoff jeans, a ratty old college sweatshirt, and flip-flops won't work for a night at the symphony!) If you don't have a keen sense for style, check out TV shows and magazines on the subject for ideas. You will notice that conservative always wins over flashy and overly revealing. I'm not saying that you ought to spend a ton of money on clothes. Decide what is stylish and right for your personality, and then start adding to your wardrobe in accordance with what you can afford.

5. *Beware of over-accessorizing.* You're the main attraction — your smile and laugh, your personality, your pleasant nature. So don't clutter up the vision with excessive jewelry and accessories that are more distracting than attractive. Unless you're going to a costume party together, simple and understated accessories are the way to go. If the bauble or bangle gets more attention than you do, lose it.

6. *Take care of your hair.* Take another look at your picture in the old high school yearbook. If your hairstyle today is the same as in the picture, a new style, length, and possibly color are in order. So go for it. This could be the single most important appearance tip you receive. The way you care for your hair can change everything.

7. *Be purposeful with your eyewear.* If contacts or surgery are not options for you and you must wear glasses, do treat yourself to a pair of really cool frames that a friend

helps you pick out — someone who's not afraid to say, "No way! Those frames put the 'ugh' in ugly."

8. *Shoot for a million-dollar smile.* There's more to dental and breath care than regular brushing and flossing. See your dentist for periodic cleanings, exams, and repairs. And it's time to stop ragging on your parents for not taking you to the orthodontist when you were a kid. Suck it up and make the appointment to get your crooked teeth straightened. A year or two with retainers or braces can give you a million-dollar smile for decades.

9. *Watch what you eat.* Obviously, there's a correlation between making a positive impression on people and diet. You know the drill on eating right: watch calories and portion sizes, balance the food groups, go easy on the Twinkies, etc. But you also may want to consider seeing a licensed nutritionist to make sure you're eating the right kinds of foods for your metabolism. And when you are out to eat with a date, don't go overboard on your favorite foods. How about trying your date's favorite food for a change? And don't forget that gassy foods can really spoil a date. (If you can't avoid them, then be sure to stay away from open flames!)

10. *Be fit and your clothes will fit.* Along with proper diet, regular exercise is vital to your health and is a big plus to a positive impression. Besides, a workout is a great way to spend time with someone you like.

You are somebody worth meeting, worth knowing, and worth dating. Attending to your appearance in these ways is one clear way of issuing an invitation to discover just how "worth it" you really are.

Behavior is important

Your behavior — how you conduct yourself — is essential to making a good first impression. I can sum it up in seven letters: *R-E-S-P-E-C-T.* It's just common sense to treat any date or person you meet with respect. You're not test-driving a car or trying on clothes at the mall. You're connecting with a person who has feelings, expectations, hopes, and fears just like you. Respect all people as persons of infinite worth and value, because that's who they are. Here are ten important ways to demonstrate respect in a dating relationship or any relationship:

1. *Don't be late.* You may not be able to tell by looking at them, but people who are habitually late are usually egocentric, selfish, procrastinating, borderline personality disorder people who are so into themselves they don't care enough about others to deal with their issues. Now, is this the type of person you really want to spend the rest of your life with? I didn't think so. Being habitually late is not just a bad first impression; it's a bad sign of things to come. Think twice about a serious relationship with such a person. As for you, make it your habit to be on time for dates, appointments, and so on. If you're unavoidably detained, call and explain. But if you fit into the category of "habitually late," you don't need a better watch, you need counseling.

2. *Focus on your date.* If the focus of your conversations is all about you — your stories, your problems, your needs, your wants — you're wasting a lot of money inviting somebody to go out with you. Respect means directing

your focus to the other person. Don't over-plan your date
or tell so much about yourself that you miss the adventure
and fun of connecting with and drawing out the other
person.

3. *Apply no pressure.* Casey invited Jen to the County Fair
   assuming that she enjoys roller coasters and other thrill
   rides as much as he does. Jen didn't say anything, but
   after one spinning, twirling ride Casey could tell that
   she tolerated it more than enjoyed it. "Hey," he said, "I
   hear there are some great exhibits this year. Let's check
   them out." Jen really enjoyed the livestock exhibits. They
   never got back to the crazy rides. Nice going, Casey! It's
   respectful to avoid things that might cause the person
   you're with to feel awkward or out of place. So don't
   pressure your dates to do anything they don't want to do,
   can't do, or are embarrassed doing.

4. *Be yourself.* Don't put on a phony act trying to impress
   your date or your date's friends. Just be who you are
   within the bounds of propriety. Nobody wins when you
   fake it to the point that the other person likes the fake self
   you created more than the real you.

5. *Make it fun.* Molly wasn't very coordinated, but she
   thought playing putt-putt golf with Raul would be fun. On
   their first hole, she lucked out and shot a par three while
   Raul, who played a lot of golf, shot a five. Molly dropped a
   few more lucky putts, but no matter how hard Raul tried
   he couldn't break par. On the fifth hole Molly sunk a hole
   in one and was elated. But Raul was in a very bad mood
   for the rest of the evening. Don't come into a date with a
   hard and fast personal agenda of things you want do. Just

relax, enjoy the moment, and make sure to focus on the other person and what that person has to say and wants to do.

6. *Tell me about yourself.* Always be ready to ask non-prying questions to draw out the other person's history, interests, work, background, etc. And be ready to answer the same questions yourself, if asked. Below are a bunch of good conversation starters to keep in mind. Please don't feel duty-bound to work through the whole list in one date; just select a few. And don't use these questions like a police interrogation or force them to avoid uncomfortable moments of silence. Let the questions come out naturally in the course of your time together. You may even preload the question with something like, "This may sound kind of random, but I'm interested to know ..." Then try one of these:

- *Where were you born and raised?*
- *Tell me about your family.*
- *Which of your parents are you more like? In what ways?*
- *What kinds of music and movies do you like?*
- *Tell me about your work.*
- *Where else have you lived?*
- *What is your favorite thing to do?*
- *What are you passionate about?*
- *Tell me about a time when you prayed for something. What was the answer?*
- *Where have you traveled in the world or where would you like to travel?*
- *Tell me about your concept of God and your journey of faith.*

- *When you want to celebrate with a great dinner out, where do you go and what do you order?*
- *What do you see yourself doing in ten years? Twenty years?*
- *Where do you see yourself living in ten years? Twenty years?*
- *When you were a kid, which adults in your life made the greatest impact on you?*
- *What are your hobbies or pastimes?*
- *Tell me about one life-changing event in your life so far.*
- *What would you do if you won the lottery?*
- *Are you a glass-half-full or glass-half-empty kind of person?*
- *What is your most prized possession?*

7. *Nose out.* How would you feel if a new person in your life asked you point blank how much money you made, whether or not you were a virgin, or why your last relationship ended? This kind of prying is way too personal and out of bounds in most relationships and especially on first dates. In your attempt to get to know people, don't be nosey. People are turned off by questions and comments that are too personal or embarrassing. This includes prying about former relationships, privileged information, gossip, and so on. When in doubt, don't go there.

8. *Practice common courtesy.* Everyone you date deserves to be treated with courtesy even if you never see the person again. I'm talking about the things your parents taught you (or tried to teach you) as a kid: always saying "please,"

"thank you," and "excuse me," apologizing for mistakes or wrongs, using good table manners (take small bites, don't talk with your mouth full, ask for dishes to be passed to you, use your napkin, etc.), let others go first, and so on. If you're unsure about the basic rules of common courtesy in relationships, search the internet for rules of common courtesy. Take what you learn to heart, and make sure your courtesy includes the use of your phone: no calling, texting, messaging, or web-surfing during a date.

9. *Keep it casual.* Take-a-Break Dates are not about getting physical, so respect your date's physical space. Don't assume that the person you are with is ready for anything more than a handshake, and definitely don't make your date an occasion to see how far you can go physically. The clearer your boundaries, the safer you and your date will be and feel in the relationship, and the better your chance for observing how you both respond to these physical boundaries.

10. *Be truthful.* A few common lines that may be heard at the end of a date are, "Hey, I had a great time," "Let's do this again," and "I'll call you." Sadly, they are often empty words used by people who don't really mean them. It's important to respect the people you date by being truthful, even if you don't have a good time, don't want to date this person again, and don't intend to call. Speak the truth with tact and kindness, but don't mislead anyone with statements or promises you don't mean.

When you approach dating with respect for the people you meet and spend time with, you can feel positive even when people don't live up to your expectations. There's another area where being proactive will serve you well in your dating relationships. That area is your personal safety.

Have fun but be safe

If the person you're going to be with is someone you don't know well, it is wise to be aware and alert to your own safety needs. I don't have to remind you of the kinds of horrible things that can happen on dates when an unsuspecting and friendly person fails to put safeguards in place. I want to alert you to two potential danger zones in dating and how to stay out of those zones. And if the person you're interested in objects to any of your safety measures, just say, "No, thanks," in as many ways as you must to make yourself clear. After that, just walk away.

First, you need to establish safeguards that help you avoid physical harm at the hands of someone you don't know much about. I'm talking about the potential danger of physical and sexual assault and anything that opens the door to them. This caution may apply primarily to women, but I urge men not to skip this section. You can help the women you date to feel comfortable and secure in your company if you proactively establish and observe the guidelines I offer to women.

Don't rush the first date. The more you know about someone new before you go out, the better. Chat on the phone a few times or exchange texts and emails. Talk to other people to get a reading on this person's character, reputation, etc. Gaining a little information ahead of time may convince you that being with this person is okay — or that it is a bad idea.

Even when you feel comfortable about what you learn, consider meeting your date at a neutral location instead of being picked up at your residence. You may also want to insist that your first date include another couple or a small group of friends. In order not to feel obligated to this person, insist on paying your share of the cost of the date — your meal, your ticket to the concert, and so on. And it's always a good idea to let someone — a trusted friend, a parent or sibling, your roommate, maybe even a cop or body builder friend — know where you will be and the name of the person you are meeting there.

Second, you need to establish boundaries that will help you diffuse any temptation or opportunity for sex that may arise if physical attraction is strong. For example, make it a point to date only in public places where other people will be close by. And if your date suggests that the two of you go somewhere secluded, say, "No way, nowhere, no how."

Establish — and announce clearly to your date — a curfew for the date. And make sure your trusted friend or roommate knows about it so you can be held accountable. Don't let the date drag into the wee hours of tomorrow. When you stay out extra late you are more fatigued and vulnerable and there are fewer people around in case you need encouragement to do the right thing. Extend the curfew only if you're having fun *and* feel completely safe and in control. If it doesn't feel right or you don't feel safe, just say no and bring the curtain down on the date early.

I'm not trying to scare you or induce paranoia toward anyone you may date. But level-headed caution and a willingness to err on that side if necessary may save you from an unwanted episode of great pain.

Be open to an open door ... or to a closed one

How can you know if the person you spent time with is someone you want to see again? You will likely have a gut feeling about this, but it's always good to check those feelings against some measurable data. The following two sections will help you discern if the door to future times together should be left open or quickly closed.

Is the door swinging open?

You may be looking at an open door to an ongoing relationship if the other person demonstrated that he or she was very much looking forward to being with you, and was pleasant, engaging, enthused, excited, and happy to be with you once you were on the date. Also, consider whether or not he or she was appropriately dressed, well-groomed, smelled good, and was downright likable, without making a seductive move on you.

You can also be encouraged if your date was as much interested in conversation and getting to know you as you were in getting to know him or her. Did your date maintain good eye contact, ask interesting questions, and seem more into you than in what the two of you were doing? It's a good sign if the other person was positive or at least respectful in comments about other people, including family members, roommates, friends, and dating relationships — ignoring the opportunity to trash people verbally.

It's a big plus if the other person thanks you for taking the time to arrange the date, expresses appreciation for specific things (coffee was great, nice restaurant, hiking trail was an enjoyable challenge, etc.), and concludes with a sincere, "I had a great time and enjoyed getting better acquainted with you."

Don't get me wrong, all these positive traits and behaviors don't automatically mean you've met Mr. or Ms. Right. But you have to admit that this person is ahead of the curve and worthy of potential friendship or something more serious down the road.

Or is the door slamming shut?

It may be best to let the door to a relationship close if the other person failed to compliment (or worse yet, was critical of) your appearance, choice of activities, ideas and suggestions, and any other way you tried to help him or her have a good time. And things are not looking up for you if your date was clueless about courtesy and good manners, didn't care if you were having a good time or not, and was a total slob only interested in pleasing himself (or herself).

You probably should back away if you couldn't find any points of common interest between you — Democrat vs. Republican, country music vs. jazz, double shot Americano vs. Folgers decaf, vegetarian vs. meat-eater, altruism vs. hedonism, etc. Ditto if your date clearly violated your physical space through excessive or inappropriate touching, pressure for a kiss, bad breath or body odor, or undressing you with his or her eyes. And you can say *sayonara* to this date if while you were together the other person was taking calls, leaving or checking voicemails, texting or returning texts, and talking to everyone in the restaurant except you.

You're under no obligation to date people like this again or try to reform or fix their problems. Chalk those dating adventures up to experience and walk away. You deserve better, so turn your attentions elsewhere.

Now that you have some Take-a-Break Dating basics under your belt, it's time to pay attention to the kinds of people you should avoid dating again and should certainly avoid marrying ... unless and until some major changes are evident in their pathological, relationship-crushing behaviors.

4

Red-Flag People to Avoid Dating and Marrying

Once Wendy laid eyes on Josh at a club near her house, she had a hard time looking elsewhere. Everything about this guy's appearance — cool clothes, good looks, trim build, and a smile that could accelerate global warming — shouted out confidence, strength, success, adventure, and fun. Wendy noticed during the evening how he entertained his dance partners with conversation, wit, and laughter. And he danced like a pro. *Why haven't I met this guy before?* she thought.

Near the end of the evening Josh crossed the room and asked Wendy to dance. He wanted to know all about her. Held by his attentive gaze and magnetic charm, Wendy was all too happy to tell him. After a couple of dances they sat down over coffee to continue getting acquainted. In response to Wendy's questions, Josh explained that he was new in the city after having worked in Germany for a few years — a State Department job, he explained. He also told her about his growing faith, his graduate degrees in European history and political science, the sailboat he was refurbishing, and his volunteer work at a downtown mission.

"Maybe you would like to go sailing with me sometime," he added. Wendy eagerly agreed, hoping there would be other dates too. This was the Prince Charming she had been waiting for. Josh seemed perfect for her in every way because, well, he was just perfect! (If you can't see that this girl is headed toward a train wreck of disappointment, you need new contacts.) Wendy was not prepared for the big, big shock that was about to blindside her.

When you start venturing out and making connections with new people, you meet all kinds. You likely can't date every eligible prospect you meet, and you probably don't want to. So how do you decide which of them to date, which to engage as friends only, and which to walk away from while muttering under your breath, "No way, Jose!" Sometimes you won't know the answer until you've been around a person once or twice. But you can learn a lot about potential dates through observation and conversation before you ever go out with them.

Here are ten negative traits that should wave a red flag of danger when you observe them in someone you meet or date. I'm not saying that these people are incapable of growth, healing, and change. But these negative issues can only be repaired with significant effort on the part of those who suffer from them. Don't think for a moment that you can change a person with these traits.

You will do better to keep looking than to invest a lot of time with Red-Flag People who exhibit the following ten characteristics:

■ 1. Just Too Good to Be True

There's an old saying: "If something seems too good to be true, it probably is." We are hesitant to pay good money for what seem to be "perfect" cars or condos or cameras, advertised at prices just too low to believe. Yet a lot of singles are far less cautious about developing long-term relationships (or hoping to) with those who seem "just perfect."

Wendy dated Josh for six "perfect" weeks before she found out from a friend that Josh was indeed too good to be true. He didn't work in Germany for three years; he was in prison in another state on drug charges. Everything else he said about himself was "exaggerated" too, including the sailboat that was "not quite ready" for their sailing trip, his higher education, and a growing faith. Josh's polished public persona was merely a façade covering an elaborate deception.

People who seem too good to be true usually are. Here are several clues that a person may be living out a deception. He or she:

- Puts on an act to make a good impression.
- Exaggerates the positive and covers up the negative about herself (or himself).
- Explains away (or outright lies about) anything that comes across in a negative light.
- Resists admitting any faults or failures.
- Seems not to have a care in the world.
- Knows what buttons to push to get you to respond the way he or she wants.
- Tells you too much too soon — such as expressing feelings

of love and devotion as if you've known each other in another lifetime.

- Is strangely secretive or involved in something "magnificent" that can't be shared.

- Seems to be without nearby friends or family members who can validate or refute his or her facts or claims.

An old song says, "Ain't nothing like the real thing." Make sure the people you date are the real thing: down to earth, genuine, transparent, honest, and truthful. If you follow the guidelines written previously, especially those that pertain to taking your time and never acting out of desperation, you have a very good chance of finding the real thing.

■ 2. Ability to Consume Vast Quantities of Something

Beware of the person trapped in addictions, capable of seriously damaging or disabling a relationship. I'm not just talking about the big ones we always hear about: drugs, alcohol, gambling, food, sex, or porn. Any activity, substance, object, or behavior that is a controlling focus of a person's life can be an addiction. And all addictive behaviors disrupt and poison relationships. When you're in a relationship with an addict, his or her addiction will always take priority over you.

In general, addiction and dependency are characterized by a way higher tolerance for something than most people have (or can handle), a need for increasing amounts of it to produce the same effect, and a need to continue even when it damages the relationship and hurts the other person. There will be a noticeable experience of withdrawal when the person tries to quit and/or a driving need to get back to whatever it was. And whatever shame there is associated with this extreme behavior will eventually die away. It will astound you that this person does what he or she does without feeling bad about it. (Often these bad feelings are there but are deeply buried beneath the surface.)

How can you recognize addictions that can torment a relationship but are less obvious than drugs or porn and perhaps even socially acceptable in some circles? Think about Hannah, for example. Jered thought she was addicted to her Blackberry because when they were out together she was constantly checking for texts, tweets, voicemail, and email and calling friends, her mother, and her sisters. But Hannah's mobile device was only a means to an end. Her behavior indicated an unhealthy need for (and dependence upon) attention and approval from others and an inability to connect with Jared, kind of like someone who is codependent. She could not get through a date without reaching for her phone every five minutes. Jared couldn't compete with so many people, so he stopped dating Hannah.

Angelo's workload, clients, and career goals always take priority over other relationships and activities. Can you say "workaholic"? Angelo's addiction to achievement and success was poisoning his relationship to Pam, so she walked away.

Carli is hooked on TV shopping networks and buying things she doesn't need and can't afford. She insists to others (and herself) that it's all stuff she needs (or will need in the next forty to fifty years), and her apartment is cluttered with her online purchases.

Like a lot of guys and a surprising number of women, Aaron is dominated by sporting events on TV and fantasy sports on the Internet. His weekly schedule is built around key sporting events on his fifty-six-inch flat screen. If you want to date a sports addict like Aaron, be prepared to play second string to his (or her) favorite teams and athletes. However if your friend's "addiction" is limited to Sundays — such as football games and NASCAR, just go with it ... as long as you two can get to church before the sports marathon starts.

Nobody is completely free of relatively harmless habits, traits, or compulsions. But steer clear of dating people who consistently elevate their hobbies, habits, or happenings above their relationships. You're not likely to win that competition, so drop out of the game and move on before you get hurt.

■ 3. My Way or I'll Shove You to the Byway (which should remind you to say "bye-bye")

Danny was a lot of fun to be with — as long as you did what he wanted to do. He decided where he and his dates would go, what they would do, and when and how they would do it. Some girls were fine with that, but even the most compliant of Danny's dates objected when he told them what to wear, where to sit in the restaurant, and what they should order. And when a date didn't work out to Danny's satisfaction, he simply said, "I'm done, we're leaving."

People like Danny don't seem to be controlling at first. Rather, you feel like you're being taken care of or that the person is extremely considerate, thinking of everything. The crack in the wall occurs when things do not go as this person plans or you balk at one of his or her directives. Get ready for an explosion of anger, an icy cold shoulder, or a steamroller to squash your request or suggestion. So if you sense this type of behavior, the sooner you balk, the sooner you will be free to walk.

You may not think this is a big deal. You may even like the idea of being with someone who takes charge and makes decisions. But it could be a very big deal after you say "I do." If you marry someone like Danny, there's a good chance your marriage will be haunted by some nightmares.

Your partner will make demands you can't live up to.

There will be disappointments and failures that are not your fault but for which you will be blamed.

Expect outbursts of anger from your partner you had no idea were boiling inside him or her.

Your partner will withdraw for long periods when you take a stand against his or her demands.

Your partner will make merciless demands of you but will be unwilling to go out of his or her way to do much of anything for you.

You will lose friends who will not let your partner control them as you are controlled.

Do you get the picture? This is what can happen when relationship nightmares become living, breathing realities.

Control freaks like Danny kill relationships by constantly demanding that things be done the way they want them done and manipulating you to be sure they get done that way. Their control of activities and events will eventually rob you of your life, identity, and freedom. Any date that won't relax a killer grip on you or your activities is bad news. Say to men and women like Danny, "Thanks, but no thanks." Focus your attention on people who regard you as an equal, affirm you for who you are, and accept your input and preferences without criticism.

■ 4. Worship of the Narcissistic Trinity: Me, Myself, and I

First cousin to the controlling person is the one who lives at the center of his or her own universe and expects everyone else to stay in proper orbit. This person is a taker, not a giver; self-centered rather than other-centered; and devoted to me, myself, and I. This person views everything that happens through the lens of personal needs and wants. Narcissists are like leeches, sucking the life out of relationships for their own ends.

It doesn't take long to identify self-absorbed takers. For these folks, the only acceptable kind of dates are those where they are "the expert" so they can one-up you on everything. If you like opera and this person isn't into it, you can kiss your Puccini good-bye. It's all about what he or she wants to do and eat and see and experience because this person is a self-appointed expert on, well, just about everything.

Conversation with a taker is virtually all one-sided. Anything you say will most likely just be a cue for turning the attention back to himself (or herself). For example, if you went for a drive yesterday, there's a good chance your narcissistic date will respond with something amazing that happened yesterday that makes your pleasant experience seem silly or inadequate. Takers' "conversations" are dominated by their own stories, difficulties, opinions, and so on. Anything you say only reminds them of something else they want to say.

The self-absorbed are "tellers," not "askers." Their idea of a good chat is saying what they want to say while you listen. They're not interested in finding out about you. And heaven forbid you interrupt them in an attempt to foster the give and take of a real conversation.

Don't expect takers to admit they are wrong or insensitive. Their inability to own any kind of failure or weakness is somehow linked to a mommy not giving them love in their times of weakness and a dad not being there to connect with them and save them from mommy's obsession or neglect. So prepare to shoulder the blame for anything and everything that goes wrong between you. When dating this person, expect to be belittled a little. And if for some sad reason you marry this person, you will have the sad experience of being belittled a lot.

I hope you pick up here (as in other places in this book) that in healthy relationships, both participants give and receive; neither one dominates or tries to monopolize the attention and energy. If people devalue or ignore your contribution, they are saying you're only there to serve them. You need to be with someone who values the mutual benefits of true interaction.

If you encounter a person who worships the unholy trinity of me, myself, and I, I have a trinity of letters for you: *R-U-N*.

■ 5. Spiritual Dud-Ness

If you're committed to putting God first in life and living out that commitment day by day, it's a big mistake to move forward with someone who is not similarly committed. There's no problem being friends or going out with this person a couple of times, but beyond that, forget about it. If your primary direction in life is toward God and what God wants for your life, there's just no reason to invest time into a romantic relationship with someone who has very different values from yours.

You are a spiritual creature, and being with a spiritual dud will turn your life into one compromise after another. Everything a spiritually vibrant person does is oriented in the direction of God — how you invest your time, your resources, and your abilities. A person who is not interested in God is headed in a different direction and serving another god — self, personal ambition, physical desires, or other appetites. Think about it: How can you go along with someone who is headed the other way?

He or she may not be a bad person doing bad things. This person may be wonderful, kind, and generous. You may have a lot in common and enjoy being together. But if the two of you are headed in different directions, you don't have a solid foundation for a long-term relationship. And the longer you're with this person, the more dangerous it becomes. It's like lighting the fuse on a stick of dynamite in your hand and saying, "I'll put out the fuse before it blows."

You may think that with just a little more time and love you can win over the spiritual dud to your worldview. (If that's you, you better stop dating immediately and join a convent or monastery, because that is the only place that will be safe for you!) Yes, it's possible to win someone over and it has happened. (I think it was back in the eighties that it happened last!) But it is highly unlikely. It is much better to live your faith with a-spiritual or anti-spiritual acquaintances as friends, not romantic potential life partners.

I have discovered that God is really smart, haven't you? And I believe the Bible is God's Word, so when it tells us not to be "unequally yoked" there's a good reason (2 Corinthians 6:14 KJV). God wants to give you a great life by keeping you from the heartbreak of living with someone who does not share your core values.

■ 6. Tangled and Entangled in Apron Strings

Here's another example of God's brilliance. The Bible's first instruction about marriage was given in the Garden of Eden right after God created Adam and Eve: "A man will leave his father and mother and be united to his wife, and they will become one flesh" (Genesis 2:24). Now, you need to know that when this verse was originally translated, the translators didn't know about political correctness. So even though it talks about a "man" leaving his parents to be united to his "wife," it's really talking about persons (be they wives or husbands) leaving their parents to be with their spouses. In other words, when you're maturing into a healthy adult, mommy and daddy become less and less important. Then, when you marry, your husband or wife replaces your parents as your closest human relationship.

You may wonder why this instruction about leaving parents and cleaving to spouses was needed at this early point in the human race. After all, Adam and Eve didn't have earthly parents to leave; God created them with his own bare hands. But apparently leaving parents in order to be joined to a spouse is so important to God that he put it in the Bible right up front.

And yet some people just can't pull this off. They reach young adulthood enjoying a suction-cup-tight relationship with their parents — which in some ways is a very good thing. But if they are unwilling or unable to establish a healthy, respectful independence from Mom and/or Dad, anyone else vying for their affection and commitment will face an uphill battle.

We use terms like "tied to apron strings," "mama's boy," or "daddy's girl" for people who can't leave father and mother in order to be joined to a spouse. You don't want to get emotionally involved with someone like this because this person's parent will always be a major part of the equation. Wherever you go and whatever you do, it will seem like mom or dad is in the backseat or the other room. As such, this person is not as difficult to spot as some of the others.

If you're dating someone entangled in parental apron strings, this person likely talks excessively about parents or family when you're together and may email, text, or call them several times a day. There's a good chance this person still lives with mom and dad for reasons other than being in school or in a temporary transition period. This date says things like, "I always want to live close to my parents," or "When I get married, I couldn't think of moving away."

When you have to navigate a difference of opinion, those tied to their parents in an unhealthy way always side with the views of their parents instead of yours (or anyone else's). Mom and dad were always right, so they still get the nod from their baby boy or girl.

If you're a woman, it becomes quickly apparent that you will never measure up to his mama's cooking, cleaning, decorating, nurturing, and loving. If you're a man, it becomes quickly apparent that you can never do enough or be enough or make enough money to outshine the magical power of "good old Dad." Her daddy may have never touched her inappropriately, but the term "emotional incest" may be appropriate when a woman remains tied to daddy even after marriage. And as stated above the converse is true also.

People who can't let go of their parents have little room for you. Look for someone who respects and honors their parents but lives independently — physically and emotionally — and relates to you as top priority.

■ 7. Mommy or Daddy Missing in Action

This person is the opposite of the mama's boy or daddy's girl. It's someone whose mother and/or father for some reason failed to provide the care and nurturing parents need to provide in order for kids to grow into healthy, independent adults. So these Red-Flag People are still searching for someone to take care of them. Sadly, they are equipped with "codar" (an inner radar that can pick up the signals from emotionally unhealthy people) so they can spot a codependent from miles away. They are a magnet for people who want to be caretakers (mommy or daddy) to others. These two are a match made in dysfunctional symbiotic heaven.

The problem this matchup creates is an unbalanced marriage that eventually ends in resentment and disconnection. The reason? Well, in this arrangement a man's wife is also his mother figure, and no man wants to have sex with his mother. And a mother figure is repulsed at having sex with her "baby boy." The same is true for a "father-figure" husband and his "dependent-daughter" wife. Eventually, the parent in these relationships grows tired of taking care of the child, and sleeping together just becomes too distasteful. And if you think I am exaggerating about this, just tune into *New Life Live* often enough and you will hear this exact dynamic, as weird as it is.

The most common situation for us is the smothering, mothering wife who tries to control her husband. He is repelled by the attempts at control. And he just cannot get excited about this woman he chose because the mothering is one of her most distinguishing characteristics. It seems the attraction works really well right up until the time of marriage or a year or so in. He wakes up and realizes he is married to his mom. Sometimes he doesn't wake up and realizes nothing, but the impact is the same; a huge lack of intimacy.

■ 8. The Ticked and Ticking Time Bomb

Everyone experiences anger. But a person whose anger is unresolved and uncontrolled can blow up a relationship beyond repair. Excessive anger is a big-time source of stress and disconnection in relationships. For example, people who are ticked and whose anger issues are ticking time bombs of destruction are frequently impatient, annoyed, or irritated. They are argumentative or quarrelsome with little provocation and they use withdrawal or other means to manipulate others. Don't be surprised if they shut you out with silence or play the victim role, something they do with great expertise.

These folks are no fun to be with or to have around for long. They are overly aggressive, antagonistic, or sarcastic. They are excessively jealous, competitive, and possessive. They are known to be negative and rude. Their behaviors are character-istically hostile or callous, and they are given to using words I am unwilling to list here, but many of them are made up of four letters and are most often shouted instead of used in a healthy conversation. (Many rappers would disagree with me there.)

Ticking time bombs are physically or verbally abusive. Their behaviors are often reckless or borderline violent. When in a fit of rage, they are destructive.

If you're interested in someone who evidences any of these characteristics, he or she is a ticking time bomb of unresolved anger. Stay out of a deeper relationship with this person until he or she has successfully dealt with anger issues. I have been surprised at how well angry people can resolve their issues, but it is not easy and their stubborn resistance is sometimes a flaw that is terminal in a relationship. In addition, if anger ever boils up to the point of physical intimidation, it tells you that you should've moved on long ago. Being married to a person full of rage is not a pretty picture and definitely not a picture you want to be in.

Direct your attention to people who have a healthy out-look on their anger. They release their anger without harming themselves or others, and they are able to forgive others, them-selves, and even God in order to move on in their lives.

By the way, angry people are not really angry at you. You are just a facsimile of someone they were really angry at in their past — most likely their parental past. But back then they were unable to deal with that anger by expressing it or resolving it. So you end up taking that person's place until therapy frees the angry one from the grip of the past.

■ 9. Fear off the Charts and Running Amok

You heard about the horse whisperer and what he did for that neurotic horse in the movie. And then there's the dog whisperer, hail Caesar, who seems to be a zoological genius, changing human behavior so radically that the little doggies shape up. *I encounter and help so many people wracked by their fears that I consider myself a bit of a scaredy-cat whisperer.*

No newsflash here, but everyone experiences fear. That's not all bad news because not all fear is all bad. Healthy fears help save our lives. But there are also *unhealthy* fears, and some people are so dominated by them that it really clogs up their relationships in a bad way. People under the sway of unhealthy fears tend to be controlled and consumed by them. (I warned you!)

Unhealthy fears are triggered by imagined or over-exaggerated dangers. These fears prompt people to make irrational, unwise decisions or paralyze them from making any decisions at all. Unrealistic fears may be so pervasive that fearful people spend most of their time either quietly avoiding them or loudly fighting them. And people consumed by fears are blocked from developing healthy relationships.

People dominated by unhealthy fears can profoundly damage a dating or marriage relationship. For example, if they have an unhealthy fear of not being loved, they may be driven to control others in order to make up a false sense of love. They don't end up being loved, but they end up with something that gives them a false sense of love. The controlling behavior alienates the partner so love is actually destroyed, but for a while being in control brings some sense of security which is interpreted as a form of love or the closest thing to being close to another.

Someone who is wracked with a fear of failure may stop trying new things or avoid joining in activities with others by faking an illness. A person afraid of what others think of him or her may intentionally alienate others in order to preemptively avoid the pain of rejection. Some are terrified of emotional pain in relationships to the point that they bury themselves in relief through drugs or alcohol.

Other people are so paranoid about germs and disease that their whole lives are driven by their phobia. And my favorite phobics are the people who use fear to produce drama. Every day is a drama of creating some unrealistic fear so the show can go on.

Behaviors like these reveal a person who is imprisoned by unhealthy, unrealistic fears. These Red-Flag People are not hopeless. These fears don't have to be permanent. Each of them can be transformed through working a twelve-step program or with great therapy or by participating in a support group. None of these people would be classified as Mr. or Ms. Wrong, but they are definitely Mr. or Ms. "Not Right Now."

▥ 10. Emotional Dud-Ness

Does one or more of the following descriptions give you a creepy *déjà vu* feeling?

- Whenever you talk about your feelings or ask how your date feels about something, he or she gets very quiet. "I don't want to talk about that now. Maybe later," this person will say. But later never comes.

- You're looking for a deeper sense of commitment in the relationship, but the other person seems to crave increasing freedom and flexibility.

- You yearn to dialog at a deeper level about life, goals, faith, and the future. But when you start up with the serious talk, your date shuts up or remembers something that has to be done. You would even settle for a rip-roaring shouting match over a disagreement, but the other person won't even get upset.

- In your mind, quality time in the relationship means being together, talking together, doing a project together, or playing together. For the other person, quality time means watching TV ("Don't talk while I'm watching") or doing stuff he or she needs to get done (work, chores, or anything except connecting with you at a heart-to-heart level).

- Opening up to someone about your hurts, needs, dreams, desires, yearnings, aspirations, and goals is something you have to do with a friend or relative because your partner won't go there.

If these statements describe how you feel about the person you're dating now (or most of the people you tend to date), you have a big decision to make, and you've got to make it now. Do you really want to spend your life with someone as unfeeling and uncaring as a block of granite? Are you sure you're up to a marriage in which your emotional needs and craving for connection are completely overlooked or thoroughly stonewalled? I mean, are you really salivating at the chance to invest a lifetime of love in someone who defines passion as an exotic fruit he or she thinks is too sour?

If you answered yes to any of these questions, you need therapy as badly as the Red-Flag People who exhibit these behaviors. These people are what we call "emotionally detached." Think of it this way: Like computers, we all come "preloaded" with a great capacity to connect with others at a deep level of emotion and passion. But for some people the "software" gets contaminated, and they are unwilling and unable to open themselves emotionally. Back out of the relationship and allow a counselor to start chipping away at this cold hunk of rock.

I'm not saying that Red-Flag People are bad people you must avoid like the plague. They are people with particular weaknesses, blind spots, or flaws who need love, encouragement, and, in some cases, counseling. What I *am* saying is that it is unwise to get emotionally involved with Red-Flag People unless and until they deal successfully with their issues. And that means not dating them — not now, perhaps not ever. To do so is to roll the dice with your own happiness and prospects for a fulfilling lifelong marriage. And that's just too big of a gamble.

If you're presently dating — or have ever considered dating — someone who is described in the pages of this chapter, I urge you to put those plans on hold indefinitely. Turn your attention elsewhere. Put into practice the tips I have shared with you for meeting and dating new people. I think you will be pleased about the people you meet and get to know.

You now have a picture of what I mean by carving out room in your dating life to meet and connect with others. I hope you see how Take-a-Break Dates with at least ten new people will greatly benefit you in one of two possible ways. First, by enjoying fun and face-time with people you've never dated before (and may never date again), you can be more sure than ever that you want to pursue a serious relationship (as in, "What flavor wedding cake shall we order?") with the special person you've been dating regularly. Or, second, this break may open your eyes to the person you should consider as a possible life partner — or it may open your eyes to the fact that you just haven't found that person yet. And, hey — no matter where you end up after your Break Dating adventure, you will come away from it greatly enriched by the experience. This is a terrific win-win deal for you!

So what's next? Well, when you're ready to move to the next level with the person who makes your heart go pitty-pat, it's time to amp up your dating to a new level of fun and adventure while doing some relational stretching and gaining deeper insight into each other. And that just happens to be what Phase Two is all about.

AGENDA DATES AND HOLIDAY DATES

5

Put Dating into Your Agenda ... and Vice Versa

A huge part of the Ten-Date Challenge is a series of ten dates that have a specific agenda. If you're really serious about someone, Agenda Dating will keep you from rushing into marriage with more ignorance than insight about each other. Go on ten laser-focused dates that involve both of you in situations that may test your limits but will also open your eyes to greater understanding of yourself and the person you're dating.

Agenda Dates are purposeful dates that give you and your potential mate a chance to experience each other in not-so-ordinary settings that provide extraordinary insight into each other. You may discover things about each other that you wouldn't discover any other way: he expects you to cook just like his mama; she can't stand being around kids; after the wedding tux, he's not planning to wear a tie and jacket for any event; she flies off the handle when she loses at anything from checkers to a chili cook-off. These are fun dates because they challenge you both and in some ways push the limits of your relationship by placing you in settings and situations that will help you experience each other and learn about each other in new and insightful ways.

I know what you're thinking: *I don't need to go on a bunch of dates somebody else dreamed up in order to gain insight about the person I love.* Well, let me just say that Agenda Dating is your opportunity to convince your potential future partner that you're a dating genius. Instead of the same old dates you go on (Big Mac and a movie, pizza and the demolition derby at the fairgrounds, chili dogs and a ball game), try some dates together that will actually move your relationship in the right direction (or wake you up to the need for moving in the opposite direction). I think you will thank me.

You can work through the Agenda Dates in this chapter at your own dating pace. But I urge you to regard these ten dates as an assignment and not blow them off as an option because, take my word for it, they will greatly benefit you both. You can complete your dates in ten days or ten weeks or ten months. However, my advice is to take ten months or more because it allows you a healthy amount of time to develop your relationship.

I want you to know that I'm not asking you to do something that I wouldn't do. Once Misty and I connected with each other following our break, we did some serious Agenda Dating and learned volumes about each other. Our Agenda Dates were perhaps a bit different than yours because I lead a large ministry organization. I wanted to see how my future wife would relate to the people I work with and serve. I also wanted my close friends and associates to know Misty well enough to develop an opinion about our potential together. And I wanted my mother to spend some time with her. So when New Life went off on an Alaskan cruise, Misty came along and roomed with my mother. Mom's opinion: "Everyone should be married to someone like her." People loved Misty, and she was a great fit for what I wanted to do for the rest of my life.

None of my Agenda Dates were more rewarding than going to meet Misty's parents. I discovered her father's love for music and his collection of hundreds of thousands of records from the 50s and 60s. (Music is huge in my life, so when I met my future father-in-law, I felt like I hit the music lottery!) I found Misty's mother to be a kind soul and a hard worker. I admired them both and felt comfortable with them. And it didn't hurt when they told me they were honored to have me in their home. So much about Misty made sense after I got to know her parents: her high IQ, love and knowledge of music, appreciation for movies, ability to memorize movie dialogue on one viewing, and her knack for interior decorating.

Another one of our agenda events was when Misty flew into Southern California from Indiana to attend a weekend conference where I was speaking to 15,000 women in a huge arena. She knocked me out with how beautifully and appropriately she dressed for such an event and how open she was to connecting with all of those women. Misty had never attended anything like that before, but she handled it as if she did it every weekend.

Another Agenda Date was taking our kids (hers and mine) and most of my family to Montana to ski and play in the snow. Misty was a trooper in pressure situations (such as cancelled flights) and she showed how competent she is to manage difficult challenges.

She flourished in every situation I got us into, and everything she had for me to do I loved. Our agenda-oriented dates convinced me that Misty was the woman I wanted to spend the rest of my life with, have children and raise children with, and partner with in everything I did. And everything I learned then has proven to be true now. This is why I vouch for the power of these sometimes "out of your comfort zone" Agenda Dates. And I would love to hear how your Agenda Dates turn out, especially if you learn some earth-shattering, life-changing information about your significant other and/or yourself.

■ 10 Tips for Getting the Most Out of Your Agenda Dates

1. *Get ready, get set, go.* You can start your Agenda Dates any time. You don't have to wait till the first of the year, you don't need a permission slip from your mom, and you don't need to pass *"Go."* Just select one you want to do and go for it.

2. *Don't try to set a world record.* If you race through your Agenda Dates just so you can check them off your to-do list, you're missing the point. Relax and enjoy the journey of getting to know deeply the person who may be the love of your life.

3. *You choose the order.* There's no assigned order for your ten Agenda Dates, so you can move through them in any order you want that works best for you and the one you've chosen to go through this process with.

4. *Don't skip the Holiday Dates.* Another big part of getting to know each other during this phase of the Ten-Date

Challenge are the ten Holiday Dates I ask you to complete (see chapter six). So feel free to intersperse your Agenda Dates and Holiday Dates throughout the year.

5. *Know that any date is a great date.* What if friends invite you and your significant other to a tailgate party before the big game? What if you just can't wait to go see the latest DiCaprio flick together? A lot of things you want to do won't fit the description of an Agenda Date or Holiday Date, and I'm not saying you can't do other things while you complete the Challenge. Whatever else you want to do, just go and have a great time learning even more about each other.

6. *Keep your focus in the right place.* Agenda Dates are a means for having a wonderful time with your significant other while you get to know him or her more deeply. Don't stress out over the details of getting every event just right. Keep your eyes and heart focused on this person you've fallen in love with.

7. *It's not necessary to punch a time clock.* You don't need to "qualify" an Agenda Date or Holiday Date by logging a certain amount of required time. Based on what you choose to do, some dates may take only a couple of hours while others may last half a day, an evening, or a full day. And you'll need at least a couple of days for your camping date. It's not how long the date is that counts; it's what the two of you learn about each other while you're together.

8. *Some dates won't be your cup of tea.* Some of the dates may be a big stretch for you because you don't like doing the things involved in them. If you hadn't committed to complete the Ten-Date Challenge you might not do

them at all. That's okay. Suck it up and get the most out of each date you can for you and for the one you love. Just keep reminding yourself that you may never have to do this date again. (Unless your significant other thinks it's the greatest date ever ... and I'd love to hear that conversation!)

9. *Don't overlook friends.* Go on most of these dates alone. The more you can focus on each other without needing to include others, the deeper your mutual discovery can go. But at times a double date or a date with a small group of friends is a great thing (especially the campout). It will help you discover how your significant other relates to other people in these situations. An eighty/twenty split is about right, with 80 percent of your dates being just the two of you. But if alone always leads to lust, better stick with the friends.

10. *Use the talking points.* Your Agenda and Holiday Dates will let you see each other in settings you may not otherwise experience. How does she handle living outdoors for two to three days without a hair dryer? How does he deal with whining kids who spill their drinks and won't do what they're told? Watch each other and learn. But talking about what you see, feel, like, and dislike in these date settings is even more valuable. Whatever you do, be sure to spend some time with the discussion topics suggested in these chapters for each date you go on.

■ 10 Great Dates with a Splendid Agenda

Imagine going on a date where the main activity is to entertain two kids — a seven-year-old and a four-year-old — for half a day. That's right; it's a date, but it's all about working together to show these kids a real good time while keeping them from grinding modeling clay into each other's hair or running amok in the city zoo. Got the picture? Now can you imagine what you might learn from such an experience about yourself, the person you love, and how each of you relates to little ones?

That's the big idea with Agenda Dates. I'm challenging you and the one you love to go on the ten dates below, have a great time doing them together, and see what you learn about yourselves from the experience. Are you up for the Challenge?

1. The Bon Appétit Date

Are you hoping your significant other loves to cook or help in the kitchen and is eager to take on that role in a marriage relationship? Maybe he or she hates being in the kitchen and needs a recipe just to boil water. What if your loved one envisions you as the primary cook in your future? What will it mean to your relationship if you both see yourselves as amateur chefs — or total kitchen klutzes? A cooking date will help you answer these and other questions about your biases and preferences related to cooking.

I remember when it was time for Thanksgiving, which is essentially the meal of the year. I love to cook that meal. But I also love help and wanted Misty to help me. And help she did, as well as throw in the traditional green bean casserole with the dried onion rings on top. We had a great time creating the meal together and we have loved being in the kitchen together ever since. (It is very much unlike someone else I cooked with who had to have it her way or no way. Needless to say, I moved on.)

Here are some ideas for some great Agenda Dates:

- *Home cookin'.* Invite your significant other over for a home-cooked dinner. You do the whole enchilada (or chicken *cordon bleu* or tofu chow mein, whatever) — choose the menu, prepare and serve the meal, and clean up afterward. Never done this before? Better get cracking on those recipe books. (It's all about following directions and timing — two skills that help a relationship stay healthy.)

- *Chef-in-training.* Who has the most cooking know-how, you or your significant other? That person is elected to teach the other how to cook a menu item. Do it together, so the apprentice doesn't catch the kitchen on fire! And if it doesn't turn out well, there's always Panda Express.

- *Double-team dinner.* Work together to plan and prepare a nice meal for a small group of family members or friends.

- *Progressive dinner for two.* One of you plan and prepare the first half of a meal (appetizer, soup, salad, etc.) and the other plan and prepare the second half (entrée, dessert, etc.). Then enjoy the two courses consecutively at each other's homes. (And don't forget to compliment the chefs!)

Delicious idea for a date, right? I can see your mouth watering already. Tailor the *Bon Appétit* Date to your tastes, preferences, and styles and you'll find it to be a great recipe for connecting.

The Bon Appétit Date

Here are some conversation starters you can use during or after your date to get better acquainted on the topics of food and mealtimes.

- Describe cooking and mealtimes in your home when you were a child, such as who cooked the meals, what kinds of foods your family ate, how often your family had meals together, and so on. Were family mealtimes positive experiences you would like to continue in your own family? Why or why not?

- Share your opinion and feelings about: couples and families eating meals together around a table and couples and families watching TV or a movie while they eat together.

- Which statement best describes you? "I like to try a variety of different foods prepared in different ways." Or "I prefer to eat the foods I already like prepared just how I like them."

- Who should do the meal-planning, shopping, cooking, and kitchen cleanup in a family?

- What's the most important thing you learned about each other through your cooking date?

- In what ways will you implement what you learned to benefit your relationship?

2. The Play Dress-Up Date

The agenda here is twofold: One goal is to discover how your significant other adjusts to an uncomfortable or unfamiliar situation. It is also an opportunity for you to see this person in a setting most people are going to be in, in the future. You need to know if the person you marry is willing to dress for the occasion or not. Will jeans be the stubborn resistant style to your best friend's formal wedding or any other occasion where dressing up is simply the right thing to do?

Here's your chance to dress up in your finest threads, put on your best behavior, brush up on your etiquette, and go somewhere special. Your Dress-Up Date will expose both of you to a world you may not visit very often, but for which it is good to be prepared. A fancy date like this may be a bit uncomfortable for you, but it provides a chance to see how adaptable you both are. And you will be able to answer some of the big questions of life: Does he know how to tie a tie? Does she know how to conduct herself in an elegant setting? Is he comfortable opening doors and seating her at the table?

- *Why are there three forks?* Save up for a special night out at an elegant restaurant. I'm talking about cloth napkins, candles on the table, at least two forks and spoons per place setting, crystal instead of glasses that say "Coke," and china instead of Melmac (not that there's anything wrong with Melmac ...). Extra points if there's a *maître d'* and live music.

- *To be or not to be.* If there's a nice theatre, playhouse, or concert hall within driving range, get tickets to a Broadway-style musical, Shakespearean play, the symphony, or an opera. Dress to the nines and strut your stuff for the one you love.

- *Posh party time.* How about hosting your own intimate, fancy dress party for yourselves and a group of friends? Serve fancy hors d'oeuvres. Bring in a string quartet from the local college (they're cheap). Have somebody read poetry. Won't it feel great to get back into your jeans afterward?
- *Care to dance?* Check the ballrooms or dance clubs in your area for a schedule of semiformal dances.

Maybe you're very comfortable in a suit or a gown. Or perhaps your idea of dressing up is pressing a crease in your jeans. The Play Dress-Up Date gives you an opportunity to release your inner tuxedo or satin gown and enjoy the more formal side of life.

TALK ABOUT IT

The Play Dress-Up Date

Here are some conversation starters you can use during or after your date to get better acquainted on the topics of fancy and formal.

- How comfortable (or uncomfortable) do you feel attending events where it is expected that you dress up?
- How much enjoyment do you receive from the events most people dress up for — operas, concerts, fancy dinners out, dances, and so on?

> **The Play Dress-Up Date** cont.
>
> - Which statement best reflects you?
>
>   (1) "I like dressing up in nice clothes for special occasions."
>
>   (2) "I don't mind dressing up a few times a year."
>
>   (3) "If I can't wear jeans, I don't want to go."
>
> - Where did you learn about manners and etiquette? How much emphasis was put on such things when you were growing up? On a scale of one to ten — with one being no knowledge and ten being expertise — how would you rate your knowledge and use of accepted manners and etiquette?
>
> - What's the most important thing you learned about your loved one through your Play Dress-Up Date?
>
> - In what ways will you implement what you learned to benefit your relationship?

3. The Let's-Get-Physical (But Not Sexual) Date

I remember the time I went jogging with Misty, fulfilling the requirement of the agenda to work up a sweat. I was not used to running with a female who was faster than me. So I was huffing and puffing but would not slow down or lag behind. What a relief when we stopped by the beach. I learned she was one fit lady. She learned I really wanted to be fit. We also learned neither of us was lazy or allergic to exercise, something very helpful to know if you're expecting a very active future or not so much.

For you, the idea here is to work out and work up a good sweat together. How will he react if you end up running circles around him? How will she feel if she can't keep up with you at anything you try? Will your relationship stand the test of seeing each other soaked with sweat and flushed with fatigue? Try a workout like one of the following and find out.

- *Hit the streets.* Push yourselves with a long, steady run. Be sure to have a goal to motivate you, like ending at a favorite lunch spot or an ice-cream parlor!

- *Spin cycle.* Try mountain biking or off-road trail riding. If you don't own all-terrain bikes, rent them for half a day. Or if you need a tamer cycling adventure, climb on your old Schwinns and pedal down the highway.

- *Pumping iron, buffing up.* Look for a gym where you can exercise, work out, or lift weights together. Or if working out together is already a regular part of your relationship, pick something that is not. Start training for the half-marathon. Or hit the hills for a hike with some challenging elements and a lot of time to talk about fitness.

- *Ain't no mountain high enough.* Get into the hills for some energetic hiking, trail running, rock climbing, skiing, or snowboarding.

- *Got blades?* Lace up for ice-skating, roller-skating, roller-blading, or skateboarding.

- Working up a sweat together will give you further insight into how you are working out as a couple. So have a great time ... but don't forget your deodorant!

The Let's-Get-Physical Date

Here are some conversation starters you can use during or after your date to get better acquainted on the topics of physical activity and fitness.

- Do you consider yourself a "fit and active" type person? Why or why not? Do you see the other person as this type?

- How important is it to you to be regularly involved in physical activities that get you sweaty, burn bunches of calories, and amp up your heart rate?

- Do you prefer doing physical activities such as running or working out alone, using the time to think, pray, or recharge your batteries? Or do you prefer doing these activities with others as a social outlet?

- How important is it for a couple to do the same physical activities together as opposed to pursuing different activities alone?

- What's the most important thing you learned about your loved one through your physical activity date?

- In what ways will you implement what you learned to benefit your relationship?

4. The Let's-Kid-Around Date

A lot of people never talk about kids until after the wedding. This date forces the issues. On my radio show we have had numerous calls where one person wanted a child and the other did not, and they had never even considered they might have different attitudes toward the possibility of kids. This Agenda Date eliminates that possibility happening to you. You're going to need some help on this one. Unless you have kids of your own (and does the person you're dating know about it if you do?), you'll need to borrow two or three little people, such as younger siblings, cousins, nieces or nephews, or neighborhood kids whose families you know well. Or you can volunteer yourselves for free babysitting to friends who have kids. If you can't get two or three kids, at least find one.

This date is all about you both having a good time with real, live kids. And not just for ten to fifteen minutes. I'm talking about spending half a day or an evening with the little nippers, doing something fun and keeping them safe. Are you and the one you've chosen to date ready for anything? What if a kid smart-mouths you or slops his chocolate milk all over you? How will you handle it when they stomp on your foot or start bawling for their mommies? You'll find out during a kid date like one of these:

- *Park it.* Take your chosen kids to a city park or playground for a picnic lunch and a couple hours of outdoor games.
- *Talk to the animals.* Most kids love animals, so get close to a bunch of them by visiting a city zoo, petting zoo, wild animal park, or aquarium. You can save money on food if you pack in snacks and juice boxes.

- *Cut-ups for kids.* Break out the markers, scissors, glue sticks, colored paper, and modeling clay for a few hours of crafts fun. Help them make their own greeting cards, bookmarks, picture frames, or pieces of art.
- *Ride the rails.* Does your city have a subway, metro, or commuter train system? Spend a couple hours riding the rails with your kids and seeing some of the city sights.
- *King me.* Spend a couple hours playing board games or video games or reading age-appropriate books to them.

During your kid date you might uncover some uncertainty in yourself or the other person about having kids. If you're just dating, it's no big deal. But if you're moving toward marriage and you need to have kids to feel fulfilled or just really want to have kids, don't assume the other person's uncertainty will go away. Face this issue head-on now or you may be headed for horrific regret and conflict.

The Let's-Kid-Around Date

Here are some conversation starters you can use during or after your date to get better acquainted on the topics of children and parenting.

- How comfortable (or uncomfortable) do you feel playing with and relating to school children? Preschool kids? Infants and toddlers? Teenagers?

- Do you want to have children some day? Why or why not? What prompts the most excitement in you about being a parent? What prompts the most anxiety?

- How many kids would you like to have some day? Under what conditions would you consider adoption?

- What are your opinions and feelings about the following:

  (1) stay-at-home moms or dads;

  (2) placing kids in day care;

  (3) babysitting;

  (4) physical punishment?

- What's the most important thing you learned about each other through your kids date?

- In what ways will you implement what you learned to benefit your relationship?

5. *The Get-Your-Game-Face-On Date*

Who doesn't like to have a little competition here or there? Well actually a lot of people. And in the wake of a win or a loss, some very strange reactions can come up. So here is the chance to see how well that competitive streak is worn.

Get ready to rumble! In this date you must go head-to-head in competition against each other in one or two areas where you're fairly well matched in skill. The idea is to see who's the best, the toughest, the smartest, and the sneakiest. There will be no ties; keep playing until there's a champion. How do you feel about going all out to crush your main squeeze? How will you feel if you're the big loser? Choose your weapons for a big match-up like one of these:

- *Take the field.* Lock horns in one-on-one sports such as tennis, paddle ball, ping pong, foot-racing, H-O-R-S-E, or badminton. (Somebody bring the Bengay.)

- *Deal with it.* Shuffle the deck and zero in on an exciting card game tournament — poker, gin rummy, bridge, cribbage, canasta, pinochle. Winner gets to deal one hand of fifty-two pickup.

- *Chairman of the board.* Nuke a tub of popcorn for an evening of board games like Monopoly, Risk, Trivial Pursuit, chess, or checkers. And don't forget classic word games like Scrabble, Boggle, or hangman.

- *Screen time.* Plug in your Wii or Playstation and get into a decathlon of video sports and games. How about a little wager such as "winner gets a foot rub"? (Just feet, got it?)

If losing leads to rage in your significant other, don't be foolish enough to think it's not a sign of a troubled person. Demand this issue be addressed in a counseling setting of some sort. Or be ready to lose at everything (just the way this person wants it) in order to keep the anger at bay.

The Get-Your-Game-Face-On Date

Here are some conversation starters you can use during or after your date to get better acquainted on the topics of competition in sports and life.

- On a scale of one to ten — with one being not competitive at all and ten being extremely competitive — how competitive are you at games and sports, in business, etc.? In other words, how badly do you need to win?

- Would you characterize yourself as a sore loser or a gracious loser in competition? Do you see your loved one as a sore loser or gracious loser? Give examples to back up your answers.

- When is competition between partners a positive, uniting thing? When does it become a hurtful, divisive thing?

- In what ways does competition bring out the best in you? In what ways does it reveal your "dark side"?

- What's the most important thing you learned about each other through your competition date?

- In what ways will you implement what you learned to benefit your relationship?

6. The Cup-of-Cold-Water Date

This date has a purpose beyond getting to know each other — it enables you to invest yourselves in service to others. You will learn some important things about each other — your degree of compassion for others, your perseverance in selfless work, your generosity with your time and energy, and so on. But the greatest beneficiaries of this date will be the people you bless and help by your efforts. Here are several service project ideas. Can you think of others?

- *Soup and salvation.* Volunteer to serve meals at a soup kitchen or homeless shelter in your community. It's not just about food; it's about making contact with the guests and communicating you care.

- *Elder care.* Do you know an elderly person who needs help with chores like painting, gardening, housecleaning, raking leaves, or shoveling snow? Don't ask if you can do it; just show up and get it done.

- *Bank on it.* Spend an afternoon collecting canned goods from friends and neighbors, and then deliver them to the local food bank.

- *House rules.* Habitat for Humanity or another ministry providing housing have projects going in your city to house the homeless. Sign up together to help build or refurbish homes for others.

- *Personal shopper.* Ask your church or community senior center for names of shut-ins who may need someone to do errands or shop for them. Visit some of them personally and see how you can help.

All work and no play makes for, well, a crummy date. Focusing on service is a very good thing, but don't forget to have some fun too. Think about stopping for a smoothie or an ice cream cone on the way home.

TALK ABOUT IT

The Cup-of-Cold-Water Date

Here are some conversation starters you can use during or after your date to get better acquainted on the topics of charity and serving others.

- How much of your life is currently devoted to meeting the needs of the under-resourced and disadvantaged? What role do you want volunteer work to play in your life ahead?
- What advantages might there be in partners doing service projects and volunteering together? Any disadvantages?
- Discuss your opinions and feelings about the following for married couples and families:

  (1) giving money or time regularly to a church;

  (2) giving money or time regularly to other charities;

  (3) going on short-term mission trips together.
- What's the most important thing you learned about each other through your service date?
- In what ways will you implement what you learned to benefit your relationship?

7. The "I Thought You Brought the Camp Stove" Date

This date takes you out of your normal element and keeps you out there for at least a couple of days and nights. Plan a camping trip in which you sleep (separately) in tents or under the stars, cook over a camp stove or open fire, and explore the great outdoors together. Who's better at living off the land? Can you still be happy seeing each other first thing in the morning without makeup (her), without a shave (him), and with bed hair (both)?

Your camping date might look like one of these suggestions:

- *For beginners.* Camp the weekend at a national or state facility with campsites, fire pits, flush toilets, and showers.
- *For the more adventurous.* Backpack your gear into the woods a few miles and clear your own campsite beside a river or lake. Spend three or four days doing day hikes and fishing for your dinner.
- *For hardcore campers.* Sign up for survival camping or wilderness camping.
- *For those who have access to a boat or canoe.* Load up your gear and explore a lake or river, setting up a new campsite each night.

Let me put your mind at ease: You may not enjoy sleeping on the ground or using an outhouse or a bush for a restroom, but it won't kill you. And you may just discover some things you really do like, including being with a wonderful person in the middle of God's creation. So head for the hills.

The "I Thought You Brought the Camp Stove" Date

Here are some conversation starters you can use during or after your date to get better acquainted on the topics of camping and roughing it in nature.

- What do you like about camping? What do you hate about it?
- Which of these statements best summarizes your view of camping?

  (1) "I look forward to at least one camping trip a year."

  (2) "A camping vacation every three or four years is fine with me."

  (3) "I only like indoor camping at the Holiday Inn."

- How do you usually handle a disruption in normal routine, such as sleeping in a tent and cooking outdoors instead of the comforts of home?
- Who do you think might succeed better at living off the land, you or your significant other? Why?
- What's the most important thing you learned about each other through your camping date?
- In what ways will you implement what you learned to benefit your relationship?

8. The "You Want Me to Do What?" Date

I knew Misty did not like the ocean. She loved the beach but not the ocean. To her it was a land of mystery and danger under there. So, when I asked her to go snorkeling with me in the middle of the ocean and she agreed, I learned a lot about her willingness and courage. That willingness and courage would one day lead her to learn to go scuba diving with me. Now that was above and beyond the call of duty.

Here's the scenario for this two-part date: You choose something for the two of you to do that you know the other person doesn't like to do (see the ideas below). Your significant other also chooses something you don't like to do. Then you set a date and do them both on the same day or within a week or two of each other. Will each of you participate fully even when it's something you hate? Can you learn to enjoy your loved one's activity? Can you barely tolerate it? Here are a number of love-hate possibilities:

- Sign up for a square-dancing lesson.
- Find a supervised range where you can shoot rifles or pistols at targets.
- Attend a fashion show.
- Take in an evening of boxing or wrestling at the local ring.
- Spend the afternoon weeding the garden.
- Attend a tractor pull or motocross event.
- Get out a bucket, rags, and vacuum cleaner and detail one of your cars.
- Spend an afternoon playing laser tag or paintball.
- Sit together reading books for a couple hours.

- Attend the ballet.
- Take the one you love to a chick flick or martial arts movie.

Aren't you glad I'm asking you to do this date only once? In reality, it's excellent practice because the person you end up marrying will not be a photocopy of you. It's good to learn early on to be gracious and to compromise when you're not doing your favorite things.

The "You Want Me to Do What?" Date

Here are some conversation starters you can use during or after your date to get better acquainted on the topics of pleasing others and doing things you don't like to do.

- In general, what are your favorite kinds of things to do? What kinds of things do you *not* enjoy doing that are popular with other people?
- Which statement best captures your attitude when asked to do something you really don't want to do?
  (1) "I usually do it to honor and please my friend."
  (2) "My attitude isn't the greatest but I force myself to comply."
  (3) "I find a way to get out of it or complain until my friend gives up." Which statement do you think the other person will choose for himself or herself? Why?
- What's the most important thing you learned about each other through your tolerance date?
- In what ways will you implement what you learned to benefit your relationship?

9. The Faith-and-Religion Date

On our show we often are asked if it is okay to marry someone with a different faith. The answer to that question is found in the other calls we get: calls from a miserable marriage partner who married someone with a different faith. If it's important to you, why would you marry someone who can't share it with you?

A big part of the Ten-Date Challenge is for each of you to learn about the other person's spiritual journey and to share your own journey with him or her. Do your journeys closely parallel? Are they at least compatible? If you're not on the same page spiritually, where are you?

Here are several possible ways for you to find out:

- *Your church or mine?* If you are from different churches, attend services together at both of them on the same weekend if possible — for example, early and late services Sunday morning or Saturday evening and Sunday morning services.

- *Faith stories.* Discuss your journey of faith — how it began, the highs and lows along the way, the present state of your relationship with God, and so on.

- *Word to the wise.* Spend time reading aloud a book of the Bible together and talk about what it means to you.

- *Buddhist or Baptist for a day.* Visit a church neither of you attend, one with a different liturgy and worship style. How is it different from the church (or churches) you attend? How is it similar?

Spiritual compatibility in marriage is a very big deal. Being with someone who does not share or practice the level of spirituality you do leads to emptiness. For Christians, you're instructed not to be linked with someone who is not a Christian. In the Jewish world, there is a very tough stance against marrying a non-Jew. There are reasons for this. If you want to experience the rest of your life with a soul mate, it is vital that the two of you agree on how to grow your souls and where they go when life on earth is over.

The Faith-and-Religion Date

Here are some conversation starters you can use during or after your date to get better acquainted on the topics of faith and religious practice.

- Would you say you have a positive, fulfilling relationship with God? If so, how would you describe your present relationship with God? If not, why not?

- What do you sense is God's general direction for your life, such as your life's purpose, contribution to the world, and so on? Does this direction seem compatible with God's direction for your loved one?

- Who have been your primary spiritual mentors and role models? Who occupies those roles right now?

- In your opinion, what are some of the best ways couples and family members can encourage and strengthen each other in their spiritual journey?

- What's the most important thing you learned about each other through your spiritual date?

- In what ways will you implement what you learned to benefit your relationship?

10. *The Meet-the-Parents Date*

There will come a time in your dating relationship when your loved one's parents (whose names you can't even remember right now) morph into your potential in-laws and the grandparents of your future children. Have you met this person's parents, and has he or she met yours?

Yes, you may have been formally introduced, something like, "Mom and Dad, I want you to meet Jenny, the woman I have been dating. Jenny, this is Mom and Dad." And maybe you've been the tagalong boyfriend or girlfriend at a family event or two. But have you really *met* each other's parents up close and personal? Were you able to spend "quality time" getting to know them — and letting them know you?

Go out on a Meet-the-Parents Date with each set of parents. Here are a few ideas for positive, enjoyable Meet-the-Parents dates with plenty of "face time."

For parents who live in your community ...

- Treat them to lunch or dinner out at one of their favorite spots.
- Host a dinner for them at one of your homes, and prepare the dinner yourselves. Then play a table game that allows for conversation.
- Take a picnic to the park followed by a pleasant walk.

For parents who live in another state or region ...

- Plan a trip to your parents' home so they can show your loved one some of the local sights and attractions.
- Arrange to meet the parents at a midway point for a weekend of sightseeing and getting acquainted.

- If an in-person meeting looks impossible, set up a video conference over the Internet.

When you're with your significant other's parents, take advantage of the opportunity to learn more about them and about your special date's place in their lives. Here are a few questions you might use.

- How did you meet and fall in love?
- Tell me about the day my beloved was born. What memories stand out from that day?
- What special memories do you have of your child growing up?
- What are your deepest desires and dreams for your son or daughter?

Kind of funny, isn't it, that just when people leave their fathers and mothers to be joined to their spouses (as the Bible phrases it) they inherit a second set of parents. Meeting prospective in-laws may not be near the top of your "most fun things to do in life" list. But these people are high on your significant other's list, so that makes them important to you too, if you get my drift.

TALK ABOUT IT

The Meet-the-Parents Date

Here are some conversation starters you can use during or after your date to get better acquainted on the topics of parents and in-laws.

- How nervous were you about meeting and getting acquainted with your loved one's parents? What was the source of your nervousness?

The Meet-the-Parents Date cont.

- Other than your significant other, what did you find to have in common with the parents, such as political views, hobbies, tastes in music, and so on?

- In what areas do your interests, preferences, and/or beliefs differ with those of your loved one's parents?

- What's the most important thing you learned about each other through the Meet-the-Parents Date?

- In what ways will you implement what you learned to benefit your relationship?

■

I may not know you personally, but I am so excited thinking about the ten Agenda Dates you will experience and — I believe — really enjoy. First, you're going to have so much fun doing things together, many things you have not done before. Second, you're going to learn so much about each other through these varied and challenging dates. And third, you're going to travel miles down the road toward knowing whom and when you will marry in the future.

But wait, there's more fun to be had and more wonders to learn about each other. The Ten-Date Challenge gets even better with assignments for dating through some of the fun and festive holidays of the year.

Agenda Dating
Takes a Holiday

Is Valentine's Day a total train wreck for your sweetheart if you don't show up with a heart-shaped box of gooey chocolates and a mushy greeting card? Does your squeeze expect you to get up before dawn on Easter Sunday because it's his or her tradition to attend a sunrise service — one that actually starts at (yawn) sunrise? Is it important to her on Memorial Day to visit the graves of relatives who died defending their country? Does he get stressed out and moody being around his family on Thanksgiving and Christmas?

You're about to get answers to these questions and many others. I want you to go on ten Holiday Dates (what we can call Holi-Dates) over the next four seasons. (For those who struggle with foreign languages, the word *holi-date* literally means "a date that is associated with a holiday.") That's right, in addition to and interspersed between your ten Agenda Dates, you will go on ten dates on or near ten of the year's biggest holidays. Remember the deal: The Ten-Date Challenge is about dating someone for at least a full year before you get engaged. Not-so-coincidentally, your ten Holi-Dates are scattered across the twelve months of the calendar year. So just relax and enjoy getting to know more about each other through all four seasons and their holidays. This chapter is loaded with everything you need to put these Holi-Dates together.

I'm challenging you to ten Holi-Dates so you can see and experience firsthand what the holidays really mean to your loved one and how they affect him or her. Holidays tend to bring out the best and worst in people. It's during the holidays that you may hear eye-opening statements like, "I don't believe in giving Christmas presents," "Easter and Halloween are just for the pagans," "I pinched you because it's St. Patrick's Day and you're not wearing green, dummy," and "I always get drunk on New Year's Eve." Well, I hope these are not the things you hear, but that's why you need to be around each other through a year's worth of holidays.

Your ten Holi-Dates will get you up close and personal with your loved one's holiday likes and dislikes, traditions and traumas. And he or she will get the inside story about how the holidays impact your behavior and feelings. Holi-Dates also provide some fun, creative, and unique ways to celebrate and experience these big days of the year together. Will your relationship survive what you learn about each other? It's going to save you a ton of pain and heartache to find out before you say "I do."

■ 10 Great Dates with Holiday Flair and Flavor

1. The "What Are You Doing New Year's?" Date

Start by talking about how the two of you want to spend the evening. Will you bang pots and pans at the stroke of midnight with a wild crowd of friends? Or is a quiet evening with a couple of friends more your style? Here are a few creative choices for your New Year's Date.

- *Get in the zone.* Print out copies of the time zones around the world. Start your New Year's Eve party in the late afternoon if possible: friends, food, fun and games, music, dancing, whatever. At the top of each hour, cheer in the New Year for the time zone where it just became January first.

- *Just fondue it.* So you're not a partier, but you still want to have a party. Dig up a fondue pot and accessories and invite another couple over. Sit around the pot to talk, pray, and fondue the evening away — cheese, bread, veggies, and meats. And don't forget the best part: dipping fruit chunks in melted chocolate!

- *Blow it up.* Prefer to be just a twosome on New Year's Eve? Blow up a bunch of balloons and slip a fortune-cookie sized slip of paper into each one containing a love note, a "coupon" for something (back rub, lunch out, etc.), a promise for the coming year, a Bible verse, etc. Whatever you do together, have your loved one pop a few balloons at the top of each hour and enjoy reading the note.

- *Light up the night.* Are there plenty of fireworks on New Year's Eve? I'm not just talking about your relationship; I'm talking about the *flash-crack-boom* kind up in the sky.

Bundle up, grab some lawn chairs and a thermos of hot coffee, and go watch.

The New Year's holiday is often the time for starting fresh and turning over a new leaf. I hope your New Year's date gives your relationship a fresh, positive boost in the right direction.

TALK ABOUT IT

The "What Are You Doing New Year's?" Date

Here are some conversation starters you can use during or after your date to get better acquainted on the topics related to New Year's.

- What are your highlights for the past year? Lowlights? Any big changes in your life this past year, such as a job, a move, the death of someone close to you? Any regrets?

- What do you think about New Year's resolutions? Have you ever made them and actually kept some of them? Are you making any for this year? If so, what are they? If not, why not?

- How do you think your relationship together has grown or changed during the past year?

- How has your relationship with God grown or changed in the last year?

- What are you asking God to do in your life in the New Year? What other major prayer concerns are on your heart?

- What's the most important thing you learned about each other on your New Year's date?

- In what ways will you implement what you learned to benefit your relationship?

---

2. The Hearts-and-Flowers Date

Is your gal or guy the sentimental type on Valentine's Day — candy, flowers, romantic cards and texts, candlelight dinner for two? Or will your special person come up empty-handed on Valentine's Day unless you remind him or her about a date and a gift every day for a week? Maybe one of these ideas will make the day for both of you.

- *Unleash your inner Picasso or Warhol.* Before going out to dinner, each of you come up with a handmade poster picturing things you appreciate about each other. You can do your poster with markers, paints, cut-and-paste pictures and photos — hey, just let your artistic juices run wild! After your meal, share your masterpieces with each other.

- *Who wrote the book of love?* Cuddle up with your favorite beverages and take turns reading to each other some of your favorite poems, prose, and Bible passages about love.

- *Share the love.* Whip up a special Valentine's dessert (or, if you're like me, you'll stop by the bakery). After lunch or dinner out together, drop in on another couple or family at home — dating friends, a neighbor, your pastor, etc. — to serve them the dessert.

- *Don't forget the popcorn.* Each of you rent a favorite movie and have a double feature movie night. (Guys, you can only rent a "shoot 'em up, blow 'em up" movie if there's also a love story in it.)

There's a lot more to true love than hearts and flowers and calorie-crammed treats. Your Valentine's Day date is a great opportunity to express your true feelings in ways that won't wilt or turn into adipose tissue (yeah, fat).

The Hearts-and-Flowers Date

Here are some conversation starters you can use during or after your date to get better acquainted on topics related to Valentine's Day.

- What are some of the ways our culture defines love? How do these definitions compare with the definition of love found in 1 Corinthians 13:4–8 in the Bible?

- Name a few people who truly love you. What convinces you their love is genuine?

- What do you think about PDA (Public Displays of Affection)? How comfortable do you feel holding hands in public? Cuddling? Kissing?

- What's the most important thing you learned about each other through your Valentine's date?

- In what ways will you implement what you learned to benefit your relationship?

3. The Wearin'-o-the-Green Date

You don't have to be Irish to have a good time on St. Patrick's Day; you just have to party like you're Irish. That won't be hard if the two of you kick up your heels and celebrate in a way that is just your style, and here are a few ways that might work for you:

- *Meet the saint.* Dig up a few "fast facts" about the life and work of St. Patrick. Meet your loved one for lunch or dinner and talk about this great man and what he accomplished.

- *A taste of the Emerald Isle.* Take your date out to an Irish pub or restaurant for a traditional Irish meal. Or if you're really adventurous, cook the meal together from scratch and invite a couple to eat with you. (Be sure to wear the green!)

- *From the old country.* Do you know anyone who has emigrated from Ireland? You and your loved one can take them out for coffee and ask them to tell you about their homeland and St. Patrick.

- *Mass appeal.* Attend a St. Patrick's Day mass together, even if you're not Catholic. Then stop for coffee and share what the service meant to you.

- *Green on parade.* If there's a St. Patrick's Day parade happening nearby, go enjoy it together.

On St. Patrick's Day, it doesn't really matter if you wear a green sweater, eat corned beef and cabbage, or shower with Irish Spring soap. Just make sure you treat each other in such a way that the other person feels like the bearer of a four-leaf clover.

The Wearin'-o-the-Green Date

Here are some conversation starters you can use during or after your date to get better acquainted on topics related to St. Patrick's Day.

- Do you have an Irish heritage? Tell about any Irish relatives you may have and what they're like. If you're not Irish, describe your ethnic and cultural heritage and how it impacted you growing up. How does it continue to impact you now?

- What are the most admirable qualities you find in St. Patrick? What kind of impact could someone like St. Patrick have in your world? What prevents you from being that person?

- Who are the "saints" in your life, people who have made the most positive impact on you?

- What's the most important thing you learned about each other through your St. Patrick's Day date?

- In what ways will you implement what you learned to benefit your relationship?

4. The "You're a Good Egg" Date

Easter is one of those double-barreled holidays with huge religious and commercial overtones. How will you blend the celebration of Christ's resurrection and the annual appearance of a bunny who lays chocolate eggs? I can share a few ideas:

- *Be the bunny for your honey.* Hide Easter eggs for your special someone in an unusual location, such as a barn, the roof of your apartment building, a basement, or attic. Include some hollow plastic eggs with personal messages and jelly beans tucked inside.

- *The season has a reason.* Take the person you're dating to a Lenten service (or services) you normally do not attend, such as Palm Sunday, Maundy Thursday, Good Friday, or Easter Sunrise. Go out for a meal or coffee afterward to talk about what the service meant to you.

- *A basket case.* Make up Easter baskets filled with treats for a few children you know — neighbors, a family suffering because of unemployment, kids in your church, cousins, or nieces and nephews. Have fun doing everything together: the planning, shopping, assembling, and delivering.

- *Resurrection tunes.* There's a lot of great music being performed during Holy Week. Treat your significant other to a live performance that celebrates Christ's resurrection. For an added treat, put together a "resurrection mix" CD or playlist performed by your loved one's favorite artists as a gift.

There will be a lot of rabbits around during the Easter holiday, but there's only one Redeemer. I pray your Easter date will bring you closer to the Redeemer and that your rabbits are tasty.

The "You're a Good Egg" Date

Here are some conversation starters you can use during or after your date to get better acquainted on topics related to Easter.

- How important was the Lenten season to your family when you were growing up? What are your fondest childhood Easter memories? Describe the Easter traditions you grew up with.

- How old were you when you realized the Easter bunny wasn't real? (Sorry to break the news if you didn't already know.) How did you respond when you discovered the truth?

- When did the real story of Easter become more meaningful to you than bunnies, colored eggs, and jelly beans? How have you tried to keep the death and resurrection of Christ a central part of your Easter celebration each year?

- Some people believe the resurrection of Jesus Christ is literal; others say it's just an inspiring story. What do you believe and why?

- What's the most important thing you learned about each other through your Easter date?

- In what ways will you implement what you learned to benefit your relationship?

5. The "What Are We Supposed to Remember on Memorial Day?" Date

Spring has sprung and summer is coming fast. It's getting warmer, summer breaks are starting, and there may be a summer vacation in your future. Before you get swept up in a cyclone of summer activities, get together with your honey to celebrate the memory of our fallen heroes.

- *Backyard bash.* Treat a few friends to a Memorial Day outdoor party complete with cookout and games. (And how about a water balloon war?)

- *Show your true colors.* Take the person you're dating to a Memorial Day parade. See who can come up with the best red, white, and blue outfit for the day. Bring along comfy outdoor chairs and a cooler with drinks and snacks.

- *In memory.* Attend a tribute in your community for fallen soldiers.

- *Remembering someone special.* Do you know someone who is currently in military service — relative, friend, former classmate? Together, make contact with one or more persons in the service during the season via card, letter, email, or phone to express your personal thanks.

- *Old soldiers never die.* Search out an elderly war veteran in your town who may be overlooked on Veteran's Day. You may find him/her in a retirement home, nursing home, veteran's hospital, etc. Together, go visit this veteran to express thanks for his/her sacrifice and listen to "war stories."

Amidst all the flags and festivities of this holiday, it wouldn't hurt for the two of you to offer up a prayer of thanks for the sacrifices of others and how you and your families have benefited from them.

The "What Are We Supposed to Remember on Memorial Day?" Date

Here are some conversation starters you can use during or after your date to get better acquainted on topics related to Memorial Day.

- Have you served in the military in any capacity (active duty, reserves, ROTC, etc.)? If so, talk about it.
- Talk about friends or relatives who have served in the military. Did any of them serve during a major war or conflict? Were any of them wounded or killed in combat? If so, how do you feel about their sacrifice?
- What are your feelings about your country's participation in wars around the world? Have you ever protested against your government's military decisions? Under what circumstances, if any, would you protest?
- What are some ways you can value the contributions of war veterans on a day to day basis?
- What's the most important thing you learned about each other through your Memorial Day date?
- In what ways will you implement what you learned to benefit your relationship?

6. The "I Don't Want to Be Independent on Independence Day" Date

If you experience fireworks just by being with your special person, your Fourth of July together should be extra loud and flashy. Don't miss this chance to do something fun.

- *Hit the roof.* Find a rooftop where you can watch a lot of fireworks around your town or neighborhood. Start with a picnic dinner on a portable grill — burgers, dogs, or ribs — with cold beverages and "s'mores" for dessert. Don't forget the lawn chairs and wraps for the evening chill.

- *Dive in.* Unless you live in the Southern Hemisphere, you can usually spell Fourth of July *"H-O-T."* Grab your swimsuits and take your special someone to the beach, lakeshore, water park, or public pool to beat the heat. Hey, even the backyard sprinklers will work in a pinch.

- *Marching music.* There's got to be an outdoor band concert and fireworks happening somewhere near you. Grab a handful of sparklers (if they're legal in your town) and get there early for a good seat.

- *Born on the Fourth.* If *bang-crash* and *oom-pah-pah* are not your thing on the Fourth, snuggle up with a classic movie that commemorates patriotism and independence, such as *Born on the Fourth of July, Independence Day, Avalon,* or *The Patriot.*

Isn't it great not to be alone on Independence Day? How many ways can you think of to express to your loved one how good you feel about this?

The "I Don't Want to Be Independent on Independence Day" Date

Here are some conversation starters you can use during or after your date to get better acquainted on topics related to Independence Day.

- What are you most thankful for in regard to living in this country?

- Have you ever lived in or visited a country that does not enjoy the freedoms we do? If not, do you have friends or relatives who have lived in such places? What do they say about the freedoms we enjoy?

- When is independence healthy and helpful in a romantic relationship? When is dependence healthy and helpful? Under what circumstances can independence or dependence be damaging to a relationship?

- What's the most important thing you learned about each other through your Independence Day date?

- In what ways will you implement what you learned to benefit your relationship?

7. The Last-Gasp-of-Summer Date

Shouldn't they call Labor Day "No-Labor Day"? After all, we get a nice three-day weekend off work (sorry if you're in retail or food service and don't get this time off). How will you celebrate the last gasp of summer together, even if you can't do it on the actual weekend?

- *Get away from it all.* If you both get all three days off, get the heck out of Dodge for a change of scenery and activity. How about finding a cabin in the woods or by the lake or near a ski resort (two bedrooms, of course). If the budget can't handle a vacation, try a "stay-cation" with day trips to interesting places in your area you've never seen.

- *A back-to-class act.* Are either of you headed back to school this fall? Need to move into a dorm room, stock up on supplies, visit the campus bookstore, or get new school clothes? Doing it together doubles the fun and cuts the work in half.

- *Thanks for the memories.* You had a great summer together, right? So tell the world about it. Spend an afternoon uploading all your summer pics to your blog or creating online albums for you and your friends to enjoy.

- *A fair affair.* You're right in the middle of the county and state fair season, so there's got to be one going on nearby. Do the whole deal: Ferris wheel, hot dogs and cotton candy, livestock shows, pie-baking contests, demolition derby, and country and western concerts in the arena.

The downer about Labor Day is that, when it's over, everybody goes back to work. But if you celebrate the holiday well with your special person, you'll return to the job with a happy tune in your heart and a new spring in your step.

TALK ABOUT IT

The Last-Gasp-of-Summer Date

Here are some conversation starters you can use during or after your date to get better acquainted on topics related to Labor Day.

- Do you like your current job? Why or why not? Are you in the career field you hope to stay in? If so, what are your career goals? If not, what career field do you aspire to enter some day? How will you get there?

- Do you prefer working for someone else (put in your time, get a steady paycheck) or working for yourself (flex your own hours, get paid when you do the work)? Why? Are you doing what you love now? If not, why not?

- What do you think about retirement? Have you begun planning and saving for it?

- What's the most important thing you learned about each other through your Labor Day date?

- In what ways will you implement what you learned to benefit your relationship?

8. The Trick-or-Treat Date

If you want to have a ghost of a chance with your special person this Halloween, you had better treat him or her to some fun or you might get tricked and booed.

- *You can't win if you don't enter.* Okay, so you are going together to a party and there's a prize for the best costumes. Don't wimp out — go for the gold! Come up with a killer idea and then spend an evening slurping hot cider and making the prize-winning costumes.

- *Treat the trick-or-treaters.* Decide on the home, yours or your significant other's. Work together to deck it out for Halloween night, then dress up in costumes and show the little door-knockers a great time. How about healthy treats, non-scary costumes, and a cup of coffee-to-go for parents traveling with the tricksters?

- *Helping hand.* Does your church or community center host a "Harvest Party" or "Little Saints" party for kids? The two of you could volunteer your talents to make it a big success.

- *A-maze-ing Halloween.* Google *"corn maze"* and *"hayride"* in your community. Bundle up and head over there one evening leading up to Halloween. Don't forget to take along a "treat bag" for your significant other, containing sweets or a small gift.

- *Take a treat.* Dress up in costume and spend an evening driving to the home of different friends delivering treats.

Halloween is about dressing up like someone you're not, so go ahead and don your Raggedy Ann or Raggedy Andy outfit.

But dating is about taking off masks and being who you really are. So have fun together, but be real.

TALK ABOUT IT

The Trick-or-Treat Date

Here are some conversation starters you can use during or after your date to get better acquainted on topics related to Halloween.

- How did you celebrate Halloween as a kid? Did you trick-or-treat? Attend costume parties? Eat candy until you threw up? Use the occasion to perform pranks like cow-tipping?

- Do you agree or disagree with this statement: *Halloween is a pagan holiday, and kids shouldn't celebrate it.* What are the reasons for your view?

- Do you agree or disagree with this statement: *People eat way too many sweets these days.* Are you one of those "people"? In an ideal world, how much sugar would you eat?

- What's the most important thing you learned about each other through your Halloween date?

- In what ways will you implement what you learned to benefit your relationship?

9. The Turkey Day Date

Welcome to one of the most tradition-laden holidays of the year. If you don't know how your main squeeze celebrates Thanksgiving with his or her family, you will soon find out. Learn well, my friend, or you're liable to violate a family tradition and end up banished to the kids' table.

- *Love flickers.* Big family doings may keep you apart for Thanksgiving. *Rats!* Make a date to go to the movies sometime during the weekend. Maybe even see two flicks. I mean, that's when all the good movies come out, right?

- *Thanks-doing.* Volunteer together to serve Thanksgiving meals at a mission for the homeless. Consider donating the expense of your own Thanksgiving dinner to the mission and eating leftovers.

- *Bring them in.* Throw a singles potluck supper for a few friends, neighbors, or church members who are away from family over Thanksgiving. Can you cook a turkey together and still stay in love?

- *Bright Friday.* Black Friday — you love it or hate it. Either way, transform it into Bright Friday by meeting the one you love for breakfast or brunch far away from the mall. Let the other crazies clog the stores and roads.

- *A puzzling day.* A bottomless mug of your favorite hot drinks, a sweet mix of tunes playing, warm and cozy inside (no matter what it may be like outside), and a jigsaw puzzle that could take years to finish. How's that for a great way for the two of you to enjoy a Thanksgiving weekend afternoon or evening?

Picture the pilgrims and Native Americans sitting around the table on that first Thanksgiving Day. Their feast wasn't as sumptuous as what you and I enjoy. And they didn't have a big parade and hours and hours of football to watch on TV. But I bet they were just as thankful as we are for the Father's goodness and for a significant other's love. What else do you really need on Thanksgiving?

TALK ABOUT IT

The Turkey Day Date

Here are some conversation starters you can use during or after your date to get better acquainted on topics related to Thanksgiving.

- Tell about your Thanksgiving memories and traditions when you were a kid: who you celebrated with, what you ate, games you played, places you went, etc.

- How would you finish this statement: "It really doesn't feel like Thanksgiving to me without …" (If your answer is "football," better have a backup the other person can affirm.)

- What are you thankful for? I mean, besides what *everybody* is thankful for. Talk about it together. Go deep.

- What's the most important thing you learned about each other through your Thanksgiving date?

- In what ways will you implement what you learned to benefit your relationship?

---

10. The Santa-Claus-Is-Coming-to-Town Date

Your Christmas calendar is already full of parties, school, and church programs, more parties, family get-togethers, and even more parties. If your honey gets only the leftovers of your Christmas schedule, you may find a lump of coal in your stocking.

- *Light it up.* If your community doesn't have a light-up night, another town nearby probably does. You know, when the mayor throws the switch and all the Christmas lights in town come on? It's supposed to make you want to start your Christmas shopping. Wouldn't it be fun to huddle together on a cold night and watch the town light up?

- *Let it snow.* Half the Christmas songs on the radio are about snow. So if the white stuff doesn't fall where you live, take your loved one to where there's plenty of it to sled on, throw at each other, and mold into a snowman you can pretend is Parson Brown.

- *Come and adore him.* Attend a Christmas service together you don't normally attend: a children's pageant, Service of Lessons and Carols, a Christmas cantata or concert, candlelight service, and so on. Stop for eggnog on the way home and talk about what the service meant to you.

- *Homes sweet homes.* Dress warmly one evening and stroll through the neighborhood enjoying the Christmas lights.

- *Don't sweat the sweater.* Host a Christmas party for friends and invite everyone to wear the ugliest Christmas sweater they can find. Give a prize for the "big ugly."

Someone has joked that there's really only one fruitcake

baked every year. It only seems like more because the same fruitcake is given and re-given all through the Christmas season. Sounds like the ultimate "gift that keeps on giving" to me! Let this Christmas season encourage you to remain an unending gift to your special one.

TALK ABOUT IT

The Santa-Claus-Is-Coming-to-Town Date

Here are some conversation starters you can use during or after your date to get better acquainted on topics related to Christmas.

- What childhood memories do you have about Christmas? What traditions from your childhood are still important to you now?

- How would you finish this statement: "It really doesn't feel like Christmas to me without ..."

- What was the most meaningful Christmas gift you received as a child? Why was it meaningful to you? What became of this gift?

- What was the most meaningful Christmas gift you received as an adult? Why was it meaningful to you? What became of this gift?

- What's the most important thing you learned about each other through your Christmas date?

- In what ways will you implement what you learned to benefit your relationship?

■

Unless the two of you are identical in every way (which begs the question: *"Are both of you really necessary?"*), your Agenda and Holiday Dates have uncovered some potential conflicts that would have certainly jumped up to bite you after the wedding. If some of your dates ended in hot arguments, cold shoulders, or icy stares, I'm happy for you. That's the whole idea: to bring your knotty (and naughty) issues to the surface before you take the plunge into a marriage you will end up regretting.

Issues sure came up when I first spent Christmas with Misty. Except I was the one who made the big blunder, not listening to her and being a bit dismissive of her in front of my family. So I was prepared to pay the price of that mistake for the rest of the Holiday Date or Holi-Date. The next morning I was ready for our heated discussion to continue, but I was in for a shock. She did not drag the problem into the next day. She was done when she had finished expressing her feelings the previous evening. That was when I began to agree with my mom, "Everyone should be married to someone like her."

If you proactively navigated through each of your little (or huge) tight spots to a peaceful resolution, I'm ecstatic. You're ready for the third stage of the Challenge in Phase Three.

But if after a number of Agenda Dates and Holiday Dates you feel a bit uncertain about a relationship you hoped would last forever, it's time for a timeout to reassess where you're headed. Chapter seven is a must-read for you.

When to Say "Not You" or "Not Now"

What do you do in a committed relationship when you don't know what to do? Let's say you're engaged to be married, but one morning you wake up with a gnawing discomfort deep in your heart. Something's not right, but what is it? The more you ponder it, the more you realize what's happening. You're unsettled about your future with this person you're engaged to. Some people have said things about the two of you. Other people have dropped hints. Now it's all starting to add up.

Your painful, scary emotional eruption is like a security alarm blaring inside you. It's the growing awareness that the engagement and ensuing marriage you signed up for just might not be the right thing to do. In fact, it might be the worst possible thing you could do. You're well into the engagement, but the only thing you can see ahead is a huge mistake, perhaps even a catastrophic personal crisis.

Maybe it's even worse than just being engaged. Maybe you're only a couple of days or a few hours from tying the knot, and you're finally admitting to yourself you can't go through with it.

What would you do? Would you be like some people I've

met and just charge ahead with the wedding to avoid the embarrassment and negative attention of calling it off? These people are so afraid of the negative reactions they might receive for bailing on a wedding that they will sign up for a lifetime of wondering or regret even though they know they are making a bad decision.

Or would you be like one couple I met who did an amazingly courageous thing that shocked everyone who knew them. When their wedding ceremony was about to begin, bride and groom walked together to the platform of the church and announced they had decided it was unwise for them to marry. They wept tears of sadness and great relief and asked their guests to pray for them in the days ahead.

Then the "un-bride" told the crowd that since her father had already paid for it, they wanted to turn the suddenly cancelled reception into a party. And party they did. This couple's courage, wisdom, faith, and honesty produced a positive outcome for both their lives and delivered them from the regret and remorse that would've attended their ill-advised marriage.

Does reading this story cause a sharp stab in the gut because you knew you should've called off your first wedding and did not? You're back in the dating scene because you're divorced and searching again for that special someone. I know how you feel because I made the same mistake and paid for it with years of grief and pain. I want to tell you my story to give you hope.

I also want to tell my story if you aren't married yet but are getting close. You may be dating seriously, engaged (or nearly engaged), or only weeks or days away from your actual wedding. If you have any qualms or doubts about going forward with your plans, there's probably good reason. I encourage you to shift the wedding machine into neutral and pay attention to what you're feeling. It may be just the wake-up call you need to save you the kind of heart-wrenching pain I experienced almost thirty years ago. Let me tell you about it.

■ Speeding through the Red Lights

Thirty years ago I was single and living in California, having recently moved west from Texas. Just before leaving the Lone Star State I broke off my engagement to a wonderful woman named Kay. But I was in a marrying mode. I felt alone, desperate, and incomplete, and I thought getting married would fix all that. So I got busy meeting women and looking for Ms. Right. I may have seemed like a pretty good catch to some girls, but I wasn't. I needed way more counseling than I had received. But I pushed ahead with my hurry-up plan to get married.

In way too short a time I was serious about two women. I ended up choosing one of them after her father suggested I marry his daughter. The woman I did not choose was everything I had wanted in a wife. We both sang and loved music. Her family loved me, and they were full of life and fun. But I chose the other woman.

We had a fairly short engagement because I was in a hurry. On the day before the wedding I knew I was about to make a big mistake. I was marrying the wrong person for all the wrong reasons. I went to my minister friend who was going to marry us and told him how I felt. He convinced me that my apprehension was a typical case of cold feet and urged me to go forward with the wedding. So I did.

On the morning of my wedding I went for a run on the

beach. With every stride I was more convinced that I was about to make the mistake of a lifetime. But I was too chicken to call it off. Being a big-time people-pleaser, I couldn't bear to face all the flak I would catch for dumping my bride at the altar. Instead, I used God as my excuse to go ahead with the ceremony. Here's the lie I convinced myself to believe: If God doesn't want this marriage to happen, he can and will stop it. (A few years later I wrote the book *Toxic Faith* to refute that and other false beliefs that had messed up my life and continue to mess up the lives of many others.)

Returning to the house where my mom and dad were staying, I talked about a lot of things with them. But I avoided mentioning my fear. They would've helped me do the right thing, because they had told me that this marriage was a mistake. Friends who came from Texas for the wedding had told me the same thing. They begged me to break it off and return to my former fiancée in Texas. Stubborn and arrogant, I was not about to admit that they were right. So I put on my tux, walked into the church, and got married.

The honeymoon was a disaster, as was the entire first year of our marriage. Things got better for a while, then worse, then better again. We survived infertility and Madeline was born. A baby in the house was a handy distraction from our rocky relationship until my wife could not handle my ever-growing love for Madeline. That huge part of our misery was only made worse by my detached relational style and heavy travel and speaking schedule. Regret for my mistake was my constant companion.

In our twentieth year together, after I was betrayed by her with a friend of mine, my wife filed for divorce. The marriage was quickly over, but settling all our issues took more than eight years, and the attorneys and accountants were paid hundreds of thousands of dollars as we struggled to divide our assets. I can't begin to describe the torturous pain, misery, and dread of the whole experience.

And it all could've been prevented if I had mustered the courage to end the engagement and call off the wedding. As I found out later, my wife had the same regrets. She couldn't back out of the wedding, because she was justifiably afraid of how her father would react. Her fear of Dad and my fear of conflict resulted in pain piled upon pain. If there had been a vitamin supplement with some spine in it, one of us could've taken it and both of us might have had very different lives.

I tell you this sad story to encourage you. If you have significant, persistent doubts about marrying the person in your life right now, step up and do the right thing even though it may be the tough thing. This is not the time to dismiss your feelings simply as a case of cold feet. If your feet are cold or your heart is cold or anything is cold, stop what you're doing and call the whole thing off, at least for now. Just do it.

Over the years *New Life Live* has been on the air, we have encountered just about every marriage problem you can imagine. We are no longer shocked by what we hear or the questions we are asked. No matter what issue our callers present, we almost always ask the same question: "How long did you know each other before you married?" Frequently, the answer is somewhere south of one year. That's why I'm using so much ink to drive home this point: *You need to know and date someone for a minimum of one year before engagement.* Anything less is just not enough time for the red flags to be unfurled, warning you of potential major problems ahead. You will certainly see those red flags and suffer the pitfalls after you're married, when you're filled with regret and wish you had not gone ahead with the marriage.

So save yourself the grief and pain by putting in the time and effort to really know this person before you hop down the aisle with him or her. To help you with this all-important task, here are ten ceremony stoppers that should cause you to slam on the brakes and reverse direction.

■ 10 Reasons to Postpone Engagement, Marriage, or Life in General with Someone You Really Care About

1. *FAST-TRACKING TO THE ALTAR:*
Beware of the desperate dater.

Keisha and Matthew's first date was magical, so she wasn't surprised when he called the next day to ask her out again. They kept going out, and Matthew kept calling her, sometimes several times a day. Matthew seemed like a great guy, and Keisha was blown away by his attention.

On their fourth date, Matthew gave Keisha an expensive gold chain and said, "This chain will last forever, just like us." The spendy presents kept coming and so did Matthew's veiled comments about marriage; comments like, "When two people are really in love, a long engagement is just a waste of time," and "I can't wait to be a husband and a dad." Keisha was only a little surprised when Matthew proposed to her just five months after their first date.

Matthew was a desperate dater in a big rush to find a wife. For desperate daters, dating is merely a means of getting to the altar so they can lock up the relationship before it falls apart. But desperate daters create desperate marriages, and desperate marriages don't last. So if you feel desperate to get married, you need to cool your jets and put those wedding visions on the back burner. Or if you feel pressure from your loved one to get married after less than a year of dating, the most important word in your vocabulary right now is *"postpone."* Don't succumb to the pressure. Find a friend who can help you be strong and resist the urge to give in and get hitched.

Some daters are *chronologically* desperate. There are big clocks ticking loudly in their brains urging them to find a mate before it's too late. As the weeks and months race past them, they begin to panic about being unattractive or undesirable to potential partners or growing too old to have children. This red flag often pops up on the first date when they somehow work marriage into conversation. Those who are squirming under self-imposed time pressure want to fast-forward the dating process before it's too late for them.

Some daters are *financially* desperate. Economic turmoil has knocked the fiscal legs out from under thousands of people who are now looking for marriage partners to bail them out. A common sign of financial desperation in a dating relationship is requests for loans and other kinds of financial assistance. It's amazing to me how many people will pony up a chunk of money for someone they are dating to buy a car, sign a lease, get a medical procedure, pay off loans or bills, and so on. The more serious the relationship, the more entitled both partners are to full disclosure of each other's financial status and history. If disclosure reveals debt and irresponsible spending, that's a red flag. These problems need to be addressed and resolved before marriage. Suspend wedding plans now until that happens.

Many daters are *emotionally* desperate. Some are eager to find a partner they think will be the cure for their out-of-control depression, fear, or anxiety. Others are drawn to emotionally damaged people they feel obligated to rescue and cure because they were unable to save a parent with emotional or mental problems. It's one thing to feel like helping someone like this, but it's quite another thing to marry someone as a "project." Don't move forward in this relationship as long as the person is still in serious need of therapy or medication.

Other desperate reasons for rushing into marriage may sound like this: "We've already had sex, so let's hurry up and make it legal"; "I can't wait that long to have sex"; "I'm pregnant"; "My unit is being deployed to active duty"; "We can't afford a big wedding, so let's elope to Vegas tonight"; "The sooner we get married the more money we'll save." Every one of them is a red flag, and red means *S-T-O-P*.

2. *ADDICT IN LOVE:*
Beware of the non-recovering dater.

One of my best friend's daughters married a guy who was a tee-totaler while they were dating. But once the marriage deal was sealed, he began drinking at a level that can only be described as pathological intoxication. Alcohol made him crazy and it wreaked hellish havoc on their marriage.

If you're dating someone who doesn't drink at all, you had better find out why. If he or she has a past drinking problem and is not in a recovery program, the addiction can kill your marriage like a ravenous cancer. The same is true for anyone addicted to illegal drugs or pain meds, sex or pornography, food, spending, sports, or any behavior that is excessive and out of control.

You don't need to disqualify someone as a potential mate because he or she is involved in a recovery program. But if this person is not on a recovery track before marriage, it's unlikely that marrying you will get him or her on track. This person needs to get into a twelve-step program and work that program consistently for at least a year before you consider marriage. If you don't take a firm stand before marriage, you're simply enabling evil in your loved one's life and welcoming that evil into your life. So if you've been headed toward the altar and you don't have a firm grip on this particular issue, you might consider you've been moving too fast. And if you discover there has been a problem in the past but no program has been started to help with that problem, the catastrophe of a wedding called off is much less than the disaster of living with an un-recovering addict. So back up or back down.

3. *LIVING IN LOSS:*
Beware of the under-grieved dater.

Whether it's the breakup of a previous romance, the death of a former spouse or a parent, or another major personal loss, people need time to grieve before seriously contemplating marriage. Those who are under-grieved cannot fully give themselves to a mate, because part of them remains attached to what was or what might have been. If you rush this person into marriage, you might be used as a substitute for the real medication and/or therapy needed. Properly grieving a loss allows a person to let go of the painful past and move on.

The really bad news about the under-grieved is that they attract unhealthy rescuers like wounded fish attract sharks. They are so sick and sad that anything feels better than the unrelenting pain of loss, even being with another sick person who is drawn to people in crisis. "But this sad, hurting person needs someone with compassion and care," some will say. And I say to them, okay, go ahead and marry the person who's living in loss and watch what happens. Sooner or later the person in grief will heal and become acutely aware of what has happened: He or she has been kidnapped by the rescuer, trapped, and (using another clinical term) bamboozled into marriage.

But that's not all. The rescuer is programmed to rescue. When the under-grieved person gets well, the rescuer will move on or get emotionally involved with someone else in need. Pathologically codependent rescuers also need counseling and deprogramming in order to heal.

Rather than walk down the aisle with either the under-grieved or the rescuer, you need to walk with him or her to the car. Then give that person directions to a counselor you've already taken the trouble to contact on their behalf. Why? Because you want to help this person in a positive way before marriage rather than allow yourself to become chained for life to someone who can't love you unless you're sick or they're sick. Believe me, red-flag marriages like this happen all the time. Don't let it happen to you.

4. *THE TROPHY HUNTER:*
Beware of the hard-luck dater.

A close relative to the under-grieved is the person who is on the rebound from a significant failure. Maybe this person was dumped in a relationship, terminated at work, ostracized by friends, clobbered financially, or suffered some other humiliating personal loss. The personal impact of the failure is subjective to the individual, of course, and the sicker the person, the greater the sense of devastation he or she feels over seemingly small tragedies.

The primary way this person compensates for feelings of failure is to replace failure with success. And what better way to be seen a success than to walk into a party with someone on your arm that makes you feel good and look good. Don't be that person. You may think you're the love of this person's life when in reality you are the loss-recovery medication until the new job is landed, the former flame is back, money returns, or something else happens that otherwise puts failure behind him or her.

5. *GOOD ENOUGH FOR NOW:*
Beware of the "okay but not great" dater.

Marriage is meant to be a lifetime commitment between two people, just you and your partner. That's what you sign on for the day you say "I do." It's not a temporary commitment either one of you can retract when you find someone cuter, more talented, richer, etc. I'm not talking about holding out for *the one and only* right person, because I'm convinced there's no perfectly right person for anyone. I'm talking about watching, waiting, and dating until you find a person who is as right as possible for you, way better than anyone else you know.

In the meantime, don't settle for someone who is okay but not great, someone who may be convenient but not deserving of a lifetime commitment. In fact, don't even get serious about people you date who are not up to your standards. For example, everybody is a little weird in their own way. But the right person for you will only be as weird as you can handle. If this person is too weird for you, he or she isn't right for you. Another example: Everybody is late once in a while, but can you live with someone who is late most of the time? If you like this person, maybe you had better find out why he or she is always late. In other words, search for the sources of anger that cause this person to use the clock as a weapon against the rest of the world.

How do you discover if someone is right for you? It's like I've been saying since you started reading this book: *You have to put in the time.* Date extensively to have fun with different people and to find a few who are a cut above the rest of the herd. When someone seems right for you, don't commit to marriage until you've dated for at least a full year. If you find something that irritates you in this person, be assured that it will be a huge irritation and a major problem after you both eat that wedding cake. Pull back and reassess your options. You can always change your mind and marry this person later. But only do that realizing that you're committing to him or her for life.

6. MAMA'S BOY OR DADDY'S GIRL:
Beware of the parentally enmeshed dater.

This issue is important to consider beyond just being a red flag. This is a show stopper, and the evidence may not fully come to light until final arrangements are being made for the big day. A question for women: Are you about to say yes to a mama's boy? If so, why on earth would you want to settle for being the "other woman" in your man's life? That's what you will be if you marry a mama's boy, because you're not his mama and mama is every-thing to him. Don't you wonder why he's still living at home at age forty? Or, he's not at home, just in the same neighborhood? Same thing. His mama has him under her thumb, and don't think for a minute she's going to let you take him. One reason she may be encouraging your relationship is that she sees your weakness and knows she can overpower you. Anything here ringing true for you? If so, pull that emergency brake and stop this wedding train before it departs the station on its way to pain and heartbreak.

A question for men: Are you about to say, "Will you marry me?" to daddy's little girl? If so, why would you sign on for the impossible task of trying to live up to the most important man in her life? Daddy may be everything to her because he abused her in some way. Maybe it wasn't sexual abuse (and maybe it was), but emotional incest can also badly damage little girls. And since they often assume they are at fault for their fathers' actions, these girls devote their lives to pleasing their fathers.

A daddy's girl wants to marry someone who makes her feel just like daddy does and no one else. She wants to live in dad-dy's shadow, so you had better get yourself a flashlight and a lifetime supply of batteries because his shadow will obliterate all the sunshine in your marriage. You'll also be living in your wife's shadow, and that's about as close as you will ever get to her. Why? Because you're not her daddy. If you can already feel the darkness closing in on your relationship, do an about face and run for daylight.

7. THE DEBT OF LOVE:
Beware of the financially upside-down dater.

When you marry and it's the real thing, you marry everything about that other person, including their financial status and history. Your assets and debts become the other person's assets and debts, and vice versa. That's why the wedding vows read, "For better or for worse, in sickness and in health, in poverty and in wealth ..." You can have separate checking accounts if you want, but the paychecks you bring home belong to both of you. Marriage means sharing income.

The thing you especially want to look at is the poverty part. Your partner may bring a shiny Corvette into the marriage, and that's great. But this person may also bring an avalanche of debt: school loans, an upside-down mortgage on a condo, alimony or child support, unpaid bills or taxes, gambling debts, and a $1,200-a-month payment on that 'Vette. (Doesn't look so shiny now, does it?) And if you're going to need both incomes to live on, can your special someone keep a job or does this person have a history of terminations and bad performance reviews?

I'm not saying that debt and a shaky employment history automatically mean your significant other should be voted off your marriage island. But you need to seriously consider how much of a sacrifice it will be to pay off your debts and earn an income that will keep you out of the hole. Bottom line, if financial disaster is part of your past as a couple, then financial counseling and wise counsel from the likes of Dave Ramsey need to be in your immediate future — meaning this side of the altar. If your potential marriage partner is not willing to buckle down to a sound financial plan now, it won't happen after the I do's either. You need to turn your skis in another direction because you're about to slam into a tree — and it's not a money tree.

8. THE PRESSURE COOKER:
Beware of the dater under obligation.

Prior to my first marriage, my bride and I felt pressure to marry from her strong-willed father. It's not his fault that we went through with the marriage, suffered through twenty dismally unhappy years, and eventually divorced. It was my fault for allowing his pressure to enter into my decision. And it was my wife's fault for not standing up to him and saying the marriage wouldn't work.

A marriage arranged under any kind of pressure is a marriage that will likely crumble beneath that pressure. If your parents are pressuring you to get married or to marry a certain person, or if you pick up that the person you're with is under a similar kind of pressure, it's time to knock that pot off the burner until you can make your own decision. Consider a few other ways people feel under obligation to marry ...

"My partner suffers from a terminal illness. But she wants me to go through with our wedding, even though she only has a few months to live." And here's another one: "It was the dying request of my partner's mother that he and I get married." These scenarios might jerk a bucket of tears in a sappy movie, but in real life you're just a sap to fall for such a request.

"Marriage is the only way I can get away from my overbearing parents." That's what you think. If you're old enough to marry, you're old enough to just say *sayonara* to your parents. It's time to move out from under their domination. Yes, you should honor your abusive parents (yes, such behavior is a form of abuse), but you honor them by emancipating yourself, getting emotionally healthy, and then raising your own kids without abuse.

"My boyfriend has done so much for me and is a really great person. I don't really want to marry him, but he says I owe it to him." I have one word for you, only three letters: *Run!* Okay, let me add a few more words. Don't go back or look back unless and until he cuts off his claws of obligation and proves to you that they will never grow back.

Here is what you owe to all the sick people in your life who think you should do what they want. You owe them the process and choices that lead you to becoming what they can never help you be. (If you ask me, this little paragraph is worth the price of the book.) Don't let anybody pressure you into a sick marriage. Rise above these people instead of letting them throw you under the bus. Haven't they caused you enough grief already?

9. A "REAL PEACE":
Beware of the deceived dater.

If you say to me, "I have real peace from God about marrying this person," I would probably say, "Yeah, right!" Sounds like blasphemy, doesn't it? After all, if you have "real peace from God" it's a slam-dunk, and you can move forward. Right? Wrong!

Now, don't get me wrong. God can and does give you his peace about a lot of things. You seek him, you feel his presence, and everything aligns and creates peace. But you have to be careful when it comes to the huge, emotion-charged decision of who you want to marry. What you feel may not be peace from God. Here are some not-so-great reasons you think you have "real peace" about this person or marriage.

You're in denial. For some reason you are misguided about what you know to be the truth, which is that it's a bad decision. Go to a trusted friend and ask him or her to give you a good dope slap to wake you up. Maybe your friend can also help you uncover the reason you are mistaking denial for peace.

You have a blind spot. Don't feel bad; everybody has blind spots about something. You may not be able to see this person for who he or she really is. Maybe this person is like your sick mommy or an abusive or absentee daddy, and you're attracted to him or her for all the wrong reasons. You have "peace" because your sick pick feels normal. But normal to you is subnormal to most people. Find a wise person who can serve as your seeing-eye human in your blindness.

You're self-deluded. You've convinced yourself that everything wrong with this relationship will suddenly get better

155

once you're married. If you have "peace" like this, what you really have is a "piece" of dung (dung is a biblical term). You need to find a counselor and say, "Steve Arterburn told me to tell you that I am really stupid when it comes to getting married, and that I need someone to help me because I sure can't help myself. I have convinced myself that this horror in dating will turn out okay once we are married, even though this stuff always gets worse and often unbearable after the wedding. So Steve told me to ask you to be my marriage IQ because mine fell through the floor somewhere along the way."

You have mistaken terrible for not-so-bad. Nothing could be worse than what you have now. At least that's what you think. So you feel "peace" about upgrading your life from dung to dirt. But dirt is not your destiny. You can pull out of this relationship without having to marry someone who is in nearly as bad a shape as you are — or maybe worse than you. Real peace comes with hope. And if you're hoping that a loser will make you better, well, that really isn't hope at all. It's just foolish thinking.

You are really confused. You are so confused about what to do that the only way you can settle your scrambled brain is to do what everybody else does: get married! You think you are confused now? The peace you're grasping for here will actually become a pain worse than death. (Okay, maybe not worse than death, but really bad.)

10. *STORM WARNINGS:*
Beware of the angry dater.

This is also a red flag issue that may not come out until the pressure of the ceremony creeps closer and closer. Anger, rage, bitterness, or animosity. If you see this in your loved one now, you will likely experience it during marriage in the form of physical abuse or sexual addiction. And you don't want to be there, so get out now. It's time to lace up your Nikes and race for the nearest exit. Don't be stupid enough to think you can fix this person. You can't. Only the angry person can help himself or herself, and rejecting this person because of the anger is doing that person a huge favor.

If any of the ceremony stoppers presented in this chapter begin to flutter in the breeze during your engagement or pre-engagement, call an indefinite timeout on your plans and refuse to be engaged or married to this person. A partner exhibiting one or more of these behaviors is not ready for marriage or is marrying for the wrong reasons. Moving ahead with your wedding despite these unresolved issues greatly increases your risk for a miserable marriage ending in a devastating divorce.

Take heed of this amazing passage of Scripture: "Do not be wise in your own opinion" (Romans 12:16 NKJV). Instead of relying solely on what you think or feel, find a wise person who can help you make great choices that lead to a great life.

■ It's Your Move

If you've spotted a glaring ceremony-stopping problem in your relationship, you have some major decisions to make. What are you going to do about it? How will you go about doing it? How will you tell others about it? Are you going to walk away or run for your life? Will you put your relationship on hold until you and/or the other person in the relationship get help and get better?

You could opt to stay the present course and let the chips fall where they may. But I urge you not to do that. Do the next right thing you can do. That way you will put the brakes on enabling evil. You'll put a stop to training someone else to be sick. You will put an end to depending on someone else to stay sick just so you can wear a wedding band and check the "*M*" under "marital status" at the Department of Motor Vehicles.

So buck up and show some courage. If you find yourself lacking backbone, find someone you can lean on as you forge forward through the hard choices.

PREMARITAL COUNSELING DATES

8

How to Be Sure You're Marrying the Right Person

John's sociology text and worksheets were spread out in front of him on the desk, but his mind was miles away from the college dorm and his studies. He had only one thought tonight: Emma, the girl he had been dating off and on for more than four years but seriously for the past year.

The subject of marriage had come up only three months earlier for John and Emma. They agreed that sealing the "forever after" deal might be in their future, but John wanted to be sure. And so did Emma. So they decided to take a "security break." They would date other people to gain security about the conviction that they were the best for each other.

It is interesting to me how absurd a security break seems to some people. "If you're in love, just go for it," they argue. But I have found the people pushing "go for it" seem to be those who also advocate divorce if you no longer think positive things about each other. This break is not so you can start sleeping around with other people. If that happens, then you need to postpone the engagement and see why you're both committing to an uncommitted relationship. Instead, it means you decide to be available to others, interact with others, and go on some simple dates. Anything more serious would be foolish.

So John took out a couple of girls from school, but he had a hard time not thinking about Emma when he was with them. He drummed a pencil on the open textbook. *I love Emma, can't stop thinking about her,* he admitted to himself. His next words were a whisper, like a prayer. "But how can I be sure she's the one for me?"

John suddenly stopped pencil-drumming. The thought that exploded in his brain sat him up straight and sucked all the wind out of his lungs. Seconds ticked by, then, "That's it! Of course Emma is the one! I know it!" Two months later John asked Emma to marry him and offered her a small diamond engagement ring. She eagerly accepted his proposal. Seven months after that they were married.

Now, this may seem like something I made up to make the point here. But in fact it is a true story — and John and Emma are still married and deeply in love today *after forty-seven years!* I wonder how many other couples would enjoy forty-seven years of love and security in marriage if they were willing to experience a few days and dates of insecurity.

What convinced John that Emma was the woman for him? Here's how he answers that question:

"Sitting at my desk that night, I suddenly realized that only two things could happen. Emma and I would eventually get married and spend the rest of our lives together, or we would go our separate ways and Emma would marry some other guy. That's when I knew. I couldn't bear the thought of Emma spending her life with anyone else. It was just wrong. I wanted her with me. That left me only one option:

to marry her. Lucky for me, Emma had already figured it out and was just waiting for me to come around."

John's bolt-of-lightning "knowing" that Emma was the right one for him didn't come out of nowhere. He and Emma had logged nearly five years of dating and friendship with each other. As they grew to know each other and opened their hearts to each other, the attraction gradually grew stronger. Over these many months of drawing closer, John and Emma's important questions about each other were being answered in the positive. So choosing each other as they did was as natural and right as lightning in a thunderstorm.

■ 10 Ways You Can Know You Are Marrying the Right Person

Your experience of "knowing" — whether it's a bolt out of the blue or a gradual awareness — will be unique to you. However you reach that point, it will likely be because you find your deepest, unspoken relationship questions answered in this person.

As you think about the person you've journeyed with through the Ten-Date Challenge, ask yourself the following ten questions. If you can consistently answer them in the positive, and if the one you love can also answer them in the positive about you, it's a sign you're in a good place. You have found someone worth spending your life with. However, if some of these questions raise doubts about your relationship with this person, you may need more time before you decide to make a lifetime commitment.

Keep in mind both you and the person you've been dating fall short of perfection. Your love and devotion to each other will continue to grow over time. So don't be too hard on your loved one — or yourself — if these questions call to mind areas in which you need to improve.

Use the simple exercises at the end of each section to personalize your responses to these key questions. Each of you jot down your responses on a slip of paper and then share them with each other. And remember, feeling good about these things after only one month is much different than answering in the positive after one year. That's why one year is the bare minimum for knowing a person before marrying that person.

1. Do you both feel loved?

The old proverb says, "What you do speaks so loudly that I can't hear what you say." You and your significant other should frequently hear the words "I love you" coming out of each other's mouths. But it is your loving acts and responses that will confirm and demonstrate the authenticity of those sometimes easy to say words. Love means putting each other's needs above your own. Are you consistently saying "I love you" in visible as well as verbal ways? Love in action can look something like this:

- You find sentences such as "I love you" in places like voicemails, texts, your computer's screen saver (mysteriously changed!), and sticky notes on your steering wheel or on a can of tuna in the pantry.

- You call to say you're going to be late — before you actually *are* late.

- He lets you DVR your shows on his TV.
- She's forgiving when you make a mistake or when you don't "get it."
- He always kisses you hello and good-bye, takes your hand when you walk, and hugs you for no special reason.
- You're patient to explain how to set up the GPS — for the tenth time.
- She saves the last piece of pie for you.
- You look for ways to make her life a little easier, such as taking her car for an oil change, bringing her a box of firewood, or shoveling snow off her driveway before she goes to work.
- She does your laundry and you don't mind doing hers.

Ask yourself, on a scale of one to ten — with one being "not very" and ten being "absolutely" — how much do you feel loved by the person you're in a relationship with?

How would you complete these statements?

I am aware of my significant other's love for me when ...

One new way my significant other can demonstrate his or her love to me is ...

2. Do you both feel appreciated?

To appreciate each other means to express admiration, approval, or gratitude in verbal and nonverbal ways. Are expressions of appreciation like the following becoming second nature in your relationship?

- He says "thank you" a lot and he even mentions what he's thanking you for.

- When the two of you are with family and friends, you brag about how she blesses your socks off.

- She knows your team is playing a big game on your date night, so she suggests a sports bar where the two of you can watch together while you eat.

- You find a new word in the dictionary that describes her, so you photocopy the page, circle the word with a neon marker, add a note, and leave it for her to find.

- He's polite, courteous, and mannerly — even when you're grumpy.

- When he arrives to pick you up, it always looks like he spent hours getting himself and the car ready for you.

- He listens with interest and empathy, even if you're just venting about a crummy day at work.

Ask yourself, on a scale of one to ten — with one being "not very" and ten being "absolutely" — how much do you feel appreciated by the person you're in a relationship with?

How would you complete these statements?

I am aware of my significant other's appreciation for me when ...

One new way my significant other can demonstrate his or her appreciation to me is ...

3. Do you both feel liked?

Think about it this way: If there were zero romantic attraction between the two of you, could you be friends and enjoy hanging out together? Do you have many things in common beside the obvious physical attraction? Here are a few ways you might recognize that the person you're dating really likes you.

- You don't have to be doing something with your significant other to enjoy being together.
- She tells you when you have bad breath or need a shave. She's not picking on you; she just knows you really want to look (and smell) your best.
- She's interested in all your activities, asking questions, listening, and affirming your answers.
- He's your closest confidant, someone whose opinions and advice you seek and value.
- He lets you know where he is and what he is doing and wants to know the same about you.
- She enjoys being with you even when you're just doing errands or chores.
- Her friendship and caring is unconditional. She'll do stuff for you even when you know she doesn't feel like doing it.
- When you are competing at tennis or one-on-one hoops, it's not about winning and losing but about doing something together.

Ask yourself, on a scale of one to ten — with one being "not very" and ten being "absolutely" — how much do you feel liked by the person you're in a relationship with?

How would you complete these statements?

I am aware that my significant other really likes me when …

One new way my significant other can demonstrate how much he or she likes me is …

4. Do you both feel desired?

Fortunately, there's more to a marriage relationship than being the best of friends. There is also sex. You will not just be best friends and roommates; you will be best friends and roommates who have sex within the very relationship God created it to be enjoyed in. It is perfectly normal to eagerly anticipate this element of your relationship and for your sexual desire for each other to be growing. And it's okay to be honest about your sexual feelings, even if you've committed to withhold sex until after you're married. For example:

- Your significant other reminds you often and in different ways how beautiful and desirable you are.
- You initiate a pact with your loved one not to make out in the car before saying good night because it is too great a temptation for you.
- She says she's looking forward to giving herself to you completely.
- He burns a CD of sexy love songs for you that remind him of you.
- You talk together about all you want to experience about each other on your honeymoon.
- You tell your boyfriend he's sexy and desirable beyond words and you can't wait until you can fully enjoy his body.
- She drops little hints about what she has in store for you, such as describing negligees she received at a bridal shower.

Ask yourself, on a scale of one to ten — with one being "not very" and ten being "absolutely" — how much do you feel desired by the person you're in a relationship with?

How would you complete these statements?

I am aware of my significant other's desire for me when …

One new way my significant other can demonstrate his or her desire for me is …

5. Do you both feel supported?

Support from your loved one helps you feel you're not alone in your growth and development as a person. A supportive person will not block or deter you from becoming all you can be. He or she will be your greatest encourager toward emotional, intellectual, spiritual, and relational health. Support may look like this:

- He encourages you to be an independent thinker and respects your decisions even if they differ from his.

- You frequently express confidence in the other person's abilities: "I know you can do it!" or "You are a rock star!" or "There's no stopping you!"

- He listens attentively and compassionately when you share your troubles, and he checks back with you to make sure you're okay.

- She asks what you would like her to pray about for you — and she really prays.

- Your loved one is not threatened by your successes or accomplishments.

- He offers his support and help without barging in to take over and fix things.

- You disagree respectfully, fight fair, and appreciate the

other person's perspective even when you don't get it or can't see it.

- He doesn't try to recreate you in his own image or remake you into something you're not.

Ask yourself, on a scale of one to ten — with one being "not very" and ten being "absolutely" — how much do you feel supported by the person you're in a relationship with?

How would you complete these statements?

I am aware of my significant other's support for me when ...
One new way my significant other can demonstrate his or her support to me is ...

6. Do you both feel encouraged?

When you're encouraged, you are inspired to go on and are buoyed with hope, even in painful, depressing, or defeating circumstances. A marriage is in trouble when one or both partners have to get their encouragement from someone else. Here's what encouragement can look like in a loving relationship:

- He's a team player, and he lets you know you're number one on his team.
- Even when you differ about something, you affirm each other and are agreeable about agreeing to disagree.
- He's generous with comments like, "You're great," "God loves you and so do I," and "I've got your back in this."
- He talks more about "you" and "we" than about "me." And he always has time for you.

- It's uncanny that the one you love will text an encouraging Bible verse to you just when you seem to need it most.
- She welcomes your presence whenever you show up and invites you to join her in whatever she's doing.
- You let her cry when she needs to cry, and you know not to say, "It will be okay" when it might not be.
- When you're having a bad day he shows up at your workplace with a care package from Starbucks.

Ask yourself, on a scale of one to ten — with one being "not very" and ten being "absolutely — how much do you feel encouraged by the person you're in a relationship with?

How would you complete these statements?

I am aware of my significant other's encouragement to me when ...

One new way my significant other can demonstrate his or her encouragement to me is ...

7. Do you both feel safe?

The key to feeling safe in a relationship is being assured that the other person accepts and values you 100% despite your weaknesses and failures. When your significant other values you, he or she will express it through concern and care for your safety on all levels. For example:

- He has shredded his "little black book" and deleted other girls he has dated from his contacts.
- Your loved one will never hear through anyone else what she shares with you in confidence.

- She encourages you to eat healthy foods and exercise "so you'll be around for a long, long time" — but she doesn't nag you about your habits.

- He's never, ever abusive physically, verbally, sexually, or emotionally.

- When the two of you are at her office party, she doesn't leave you to fend for yourself while she chats with the girlfriends — unless you're cool with that.

- He's into keeping you safe in every way, so he makes sure you're buckled in, he doesn't drive recklessly, and he waits until you're safely inside your apartment before he leaves.

- She introduces you proudly as her "lifetime squeeze" or "the man of my dreams" or "the guy I'm going to spend my life with."

- There are no subjects off limits for him; he's an open book. You can cry whenever you need to and he's okay with it.

Ask yourself, on a scale of one to ten — with one being "not very" and ten being "absolutely" — how much do you feel safe with the person you're in a relationship with?

How would you complete these statements?

I am aware of my significant other's concern for my safety when ...

One new way my significant other can demonstrate his or her commitment to my safety is ...

8. Do you both feel trusted?

Are you trustworthy? Has your consistent dependability earned your significant other's confidence? Can he or she rely completely on your character, ability, strength, and truth? Here's what that rock of trust might look like in your relationship:

- She likes taking you along when she shops for clothes, because you're both truthful and tactful when she asks, "How do I look?"
- You never lie to each other — not even little white ones.
- When you ask him to check the pressure in your tires, and he says he will do it, he does it — especially if you cut him a little slack on how soon.
- She tells you about everything, even about running into her old boyfriend at church and how awkward she felt.
- You are respectful with everything he entrusts to you, from his possessions to his secrets to his feelings.
- She lets you borrow her car — without a list of buts.
- She doesn't come off as jealous or nosey when you have to travel with female business associates.
- You are completely honest in what you tell him, even when the truth hurts to say or to hear.

Ask yourself, on a scale of one to ten — with one being "not very" and ten being "absolutely" — how much do you feel trusted by the person you're in a relationship with?

How would you complete these statements?

I am aware of my significant other's trust in me when ...

One new way my significant other can demonstrate his or her trust in me is ...

9. Do you both feel happy?

You may be crazy-busy juggling a full load at school, a part-time job, and maybe an internship. Your loved one has all of that plus the care of an invalid relative. And this doesn't count the pressure of a wedding date on the horizon and finding an apartment together. But no matter how crammed and stressful your lives may be, don't let it rob you of the happiness of being in love anticipating marriage. Are you purposely keeping the fun alive in ways like these?

- She turns the chore of washing your car into an all-out water fight by ambushing you with the garden hose and a big wet sponge.

- Every Monday you email each other the corniest joke you can find on the web.

- You make a point at least once a month to double-date with a couple who can always make you laugh until you cry.

- He keeps a couple of crazy hats in the trunk of the car, and sometimes the two of you will wear them into the mall just to see other people smile.

- She keeps a 1000-piece jigsaw puzzle spread out on a table. Before you go out, she challenges you to see who can find ten pieces that fit.

- Whenever you rent a movie together, you go to the comedy section for something that will make you laugh.

- You show up at her house with popcorn to pop and the board game Candy Land to play.

- She can always lighten your mood with a few well-placed tickles.

Ask yourself, on a scale of one to ten — with one being "not very" and ten being "absolutely" — how much do you feel your significant other's happiness with you?

How would you complete these statements?

I am aware of my significant other's happiness for me when …

One new way my significant other can demonstrate how happy he or she is with me is …

10. Do you both feel good about yourselves?

Your relationship should bring out the best in both of you. Your mutual love and acceptance should serve as fountains of refreshment for your self-esteem. For example:

- He's your greatest fan and your most enthusiastic cheerleader, always positive with hugs or high fives.
- She frequently compliments your appearance, clothing, disposition, hard work, dynamite kisses, etc.
- You have programmed into your calendar significant dates in your relationship, such as the anniversary of your first date and first kiss, the other's birthday and half-birthday, etc. You surprise her with a card or gift for each one.
- She brings out the best in you, and she says the same about you.
- He's generous with compliments, gifts, and affirmation and miserly with criticism and judgments.
- She gives you plenty of reasons to love yourself.

Ask yourself, on a scale of one to ten — with one being "not very" and ten being "absolutely" — how much does your significant other help you feel good about yourself?

How would you complete these statements?

My significant other helps me feel good about myself when ...
One new way my significant other can help me feel good
about myself is ...

■

One of the things I love about my life with Misty is that I can say yes to all ten of these questions. These top-ten qualities are worth the work and the wait. If they don't exist in abundance in your relationship, maybe the long-term commitment you are in should not exist either. But if after more than a year together these qualities are rich and growing in your relationship, it's a good sign you're ready for engagement.

10 Final Dates before "I Do"

Wherever you are on the journey that ends in marriage, this chapter will help you get there. If you're now engaged to be married (congratulations, by the way!), now is the perfect time to get started on the Premarital Counseling Phase of the Ten-Date Challenge. Or you may not have popped the question or seen a ring yet, but that happy prospect is glowing at you from a near horizon. Engagement is just a matter of time, so this chapter will give you a great head start on Premarital Counseling Dates. And even if you're not close to being engaged to anyone, but you're planning to eventually be married, you're smart to read up on what you will be doing some day.

◼ The Basics about Premarital Counseling

Premarital counseling is the process of gaining valuable insight about yourself, your chosen loved one, and the married life ahead of you *before* you marry. A key player in your premarital counseling will be your counselor (we'll get back to this person in a sec). Premarital counseling will help you determine if you're fit and ready for marriage right now. Next to your faith, this is the most important decision you will ever make. Value your counselor's insight and wisdom to guide your decision-making. Your counseling will also prepare you for the lifelong task of blending your individual lives together as smoothly as possible.

Now, back to your counselor. You need a professional counselor with training and experience in the field of premarital and marital counseling. Your church and/or your pastor may offer premarital counseling as part of the wedding package, and that's all well and good. But if the persons providing the counseling do not have graduate and post-grad degrees in the area of marriage and family counseling, you also need a professional for the premarital dates presented in the pages ahead.

In addition to educational background and experience, look for a counselor who comes with high recommendations from people who have received premarital counseling from him or her. Consider finding a counselor who shares your basic value system and faith perspective.

As for the ten Premarital Counseling Dates laid out in this chapter, I challenge you to complete them over a period of ten to twenty weeks. For each of the ten topics to be covered, you will need enough time to meet alone as a couple and then to meet together with your counselor for at least an hour. And since the last few weeks before your wedding day can get pretty hectic, I strongly suggest you complete your premarital counseling at least a month before the ceremony.

"How much will a counselor charge?" you may be thinking. Well, just like other professionals whose services are important to you (doctor, attorney, accountant, fitness coach, etc.), trained counselors make their living from their knowledge, skill, and experience. So be prepared to pay. The good news is that prices will vary, so shop around. Take the same view toward this expense as you do toward things like the flowers, the reception (with that awesome DJ your roommate recommended), and your honeymoon trip to Costa Rica (or your uncle's cabin in Colorado or wherever). You want everything to be just right, and you're willing to pay for what you want. And that's just for the wedding! Don't compromise on your investment in the years and decades that will follow your wedding.

The first thing you need to do is select a marriage counselor and schedule your ten counseling appointments well in advance. One appointment each week for ten consecutive weeks is ideal. Explain that you want each weekly appointment to focus on one of the ten topics from this chapter. If possible, give your counselor a copy of this book or photocopies of the pages in this chapter so he or she can prepare for discussion in these topic areas:

- Marriage Expectations
- Interests and Activities
- Role Expectations
- Personal Preferences
- Communication and Listening
- Family Dynamics and Boundaries
- Faith and Spiritual Life
- Finances
- Children and Parenting
- Sex

Second, before each scheduled appointment with your counselor, meet together as a couple for your Premarital "Counseling Date" to discuss the questions in this chapter related to the topic to be covered during your appointment. This is kind of a low key date, like meeting for coffee or a meal in a place where you can enjoy quiet conversation without interruption. Use the comments and questions in each section below to help you discuss and share your thoughts and feelings about the topic. As you talk, write down any questions and comments you want to share with your counselor when you next meet.

Third, after you've chatted up the topic with each other, meet with your counselor to get his or her take and to present any questions and concerns you may have.

▩ 10 Top Topics for Your Premarital Counseling Dates

It's a good thing you two enjoy being together because you have a lot to talk about over the next ten to twenty weeks. After all, you're on the doorstep of merging two lifetime histories; two sets of values, dreams, and goals; two busy day-to-day *modi operandi*; and two assortments of furniture, music, exercise equipment, and other stuff under one roof. When two corporations come together in merger, they employ platoons of lawyers, analysts, strategists, and advisors to assure it works. Your marriage merger depends on, well, the two of you — with a little help and encouragement from family members, friends, and a counselor or two. Like I said, you two have a lot to talk about.

I'm not saying everything you need to discuss on your Premarital Counseling Dates is covered in the ten topics treated in this chapter. But, like the big booster rockets that lift our space shuttles into orbit, these ten "biggies" will launch you well into your lifetime journey as husband and wife.

1. THERE'S NO MAGIC IN WEDDING CAKE:
Debunking unreal marriage expectations

Let's blow up a myth common among men and women heading for the altar. It goes something like this: *Getting married will solve all my problems.* That's right; some people really think stuffing a little wedding cake into each other's mouths will make life perfect, solving all your problems and conflicts.

You might find magic cake in a Disney movie, but there won't be any at your wedding. Getting married is a wonderful thing, and your wedding day will be one of the happiest of your life. But getting married doesn't automatically give you a total makeover. You and your significant other will be the same people after your vows that you were before. Any changes you hope to see in your behavior, habits, attitude, or life circumstances can only be realized when you set to work on them yourself. And the best time to start is now, before you tie the knot.

Debunking Unreal Marriage Expectations

Sit down together and talk through the following questions and any related topics that come up. Write down any questions or issues you wish to discuss further with your counselor.

- *What do you expect marriage to fix or improve for you?* For example, maybe you have been hoping the stress in your life will be lifted after marriage and you'll be a different person. Or you think being married magically means all your secret sexual tendencies and temptations will go away. Or you expect to turn over a new leaf and magically start losing the pounds you haven't been able to shed as a single. You may even be hoping your secret addictions will melt away in your new marital state.

- *What do you expect marriage to fix or improve for your partner?* For example, are you expecting your partner to make you eternally happy, to love your bluegrass music, to start waiting on you hand and foot, or to stop drinking and carousing?

- *List a few positive, realistic expectations you can share for your life together.* For example, is it okay to expect mutual acceptance, affirmation, and assistance as each of you grow through the changes and improvements you seek in yourselves?

- *What can you and your partner do to start working on the things you want to fix or improve?* Perhaps you would like to start by identifying one area where you each want to move in a direction that is healthier for yourself and your relationship.

2. CALENDARS IN COLLISION:
Blending individual interests and activities

Newlywed Jillian texted her husband, Ben, at work that her aunt was coming over that evening to bring a wedding present and eat tacos with them. He texted her to say he couldn't make it because it was poker night with the guys. She asked him to skip it for one night. Ben replied that he *never* skips poker night. The texts kept flying for five minutes as they took turns suggesting and shooting down alternate dates for Aunt Minnie to come over. Their calendars were jammed — a softball game, a baby shower, a work appointment, an art class, a favorite TV show, band practice. Jillian finally snapped off her phone. Ticked that Ben wouldn't give up his poker night, she decided to host her aunt alone. Ben's taco dinner wasn't the only thing that was cold when he got home after poker.

Jillian and Ben are having a little trouble blending their individual interests and activities since getting married. You will too unless you talk honestly about plans and expectations for your day-to-day life together. I'm not saying you have to give up your individuality and do everything together like you were conjoined twins. Marriage is not about morphing into the same person or doing only the same things. It's about evaluating your personal interests under the priority of your common interests and goals in order to build peace into your marriage.

Blending Individual Interests and Activities

Sit down together and talk through the following questions and any related topics that come up. Write down any questions or issues you wish to discuss further with your counselor.

- *What activities do you enjoy doing together?* List your common interests, such as singing in the church choir, watching movies, playing coed team sports, shopping for antiques, cooking for friends, growing an organic garden, and so on.

- *What activities do you like to do alone?* List those things you enjoy doing "solo" to clear your thoughts and charge your batteries, such as skydiving, blogging, staying late at the office to catch up, hiking, puttering in your workshop or studio, or going to the movies all by yourself.

- *How do you feel about the activities and interests you have listed?* For example, are you uneasy about your partner spending time with old friends — same sex or opposite sex — without including you? Do you wonder if your partner's hobbies or "me-time" interests (sports, social networking, online gaming, other relationships, etc.) are an addiction?

- *What is your plan for blending activities and interests so it works for both of you?* Which of your together activities are top priorities in your schedule, such as attending church together, going to bed at the same time, working out at the gym together, etc.? Which personal activities are you willing to curtail or give up in response to your partner's concerns?

3. WHO DOES WHAT?:
Clarifying role expectations

Tiffany grew up in a home where her parents did all the cleaning, including Tiffany's room. Bronson got yelled at if his room wasn't shipshape every morning before he left for school. When Tiffany and Bronson marry, who's going to make the bed and pick up the dirty socks and underwear?

Just like single life, married life comes with plenty of work that needs to get done — a paycheck to earn, a home to be maintained, meals to be prepared and cleaned up after, and so on. But who will do which jobs in your marriage? Now is the time to start talking about it.

Clarifying Role Expectations

Sit down together and talk through the following questions and any related topics that come up. Write down any questions or issues you wish to discuss further with your counselor.

- *What are your expectations for who's in charge in your marriage?* Here are a few of the more prominent views on this question. Which one best describes the home where you grew up? What do you expect "in charge" to look like in your marriage?

  - *Me Tarzan!* The husband is king and the wife is his servant. Whenever he says, "Jump!" she says, "How high?" (On her way up.)

  - *If mama ain't happy ...* The wife wears the pants in the family and brings home the bacon to a husband who does what she says.

  - *Breadwinner and homemaker.* He earns a living while she, in loving submission, takes care of the house and kiddies.

  - *Partners.* This couple values mutual respect, mutual responsibility, and mutual submission. They're not concerned about "traditional" roles.

- *Who does the household chores?* Take out the trash, clean the toilet, clear the table, load the dishwasher, pick up Fido's mess, wash the clothes — the list goes on and on. How will you divide up these many tasks? (Warning: "Not my job" is the wrong answer!)

4. *YOUR STYLE, MY STYLE:*
Making room for personal preferences

Most conflicts in marriage are not over issues of good and bad, right and wrong; they're over matters of personal preference and style. For example:

> *"For the umpteenth time, I don't like my coffee in a mug;*
> *I like it in a cup!"*

> *"Why do you crank the thermostat up to 80 degrees?*
> *Put on a sweater!"*

> *"You fold my shirts all wrong. Just let me do it!"*

It's not wrong that he prefers his boxer shorts ironed and on hangers in the closet or that she prefers sleeping in flannel PJs instead of a satin gown. It's okay if she likes to have lunch with her mother twice a week and that he goes off with the guys twice a year for a golf-your-brains-out weekend. What matters is that you understand your partner's personal preferences, accommodate them, honor them whenever possible, and amicably compromise when there's a conflict.

=== TALK ABOUT IT ===

Making Room for Personal Preferences

Sit down together and talk through the following questions and any related topics that come up. Write down any questions or issues you wish to discuss further with your counselor.

- *Are you a rooster or a night owl?* Learning about and adjusting to your partner's inner clock will go a long way to building harmony in your relationship. Here are a number of time-sensitive issues. Talk about how you can honor each other's personal preferences. For example:

– Are you an early-riser or late-sleeper — or both?

– Do you fade out at 10:00 p.m., or are you just getting amped up for another two hours?

– When are you most productive in the following activities: morning, afternoon, or evening? Exercising, thinking, reading, writing, praying, creating, getting in extra work, romancing, vegging out, napping, cleaning chores.

– Do you like to take each day and week as it comes with a lot of built-in spontaneity, or do you prefer a plan and a schedule?

• *Do you squeeze in the middle or at the end?* How are you going to handle the toothpaste tube dilemma and other personal preferences such as the following?

– Toilet lid up or down?

– Toilet tissue over or under?

– Clothes spun dry or ironed?

– Half-and-half or non-dairy creamer?

– Organic or non-organic?

– Sugar, honey, or sweetener?

– TV or no TV during dinner?

– Alcohol in the house or not?

5. *KEEP TALKING AND LISTENING:*
Opening lines of communication

One of the ongoing challenges and rewards of marriage is keeping communication open, positive, and flowing. The goal of communication with your partner is to grow in intimacy, not to win arguments, one-up your partner, dump your info load, make your point, or set your partner straight. Seek to understand your partner, not to react to what he or she says. Ask questions, listen, and keep an open mind. Ask about things that interest your partner, his or her activities, anxieties, etc. Be respectful always, even when you disagree. Avoid shaming, blaming, negativity, sarcasm, ridicule, judgment, accusations, etc. Make sure your body language is as respectful as your words and tone.

Communication training is really listening training. God gave you two ears but only one mouth. Learn to listen to your partner intently without interrupting. Whenever possible, talk face to face and eye to eye without external distractions or interruptions. Make time to talk and listen. Turn off the TV, your iPod, and your iPad. Talk while driving, eating meals, etc. Guys, your gal is probably wired for a higher word count than you are. Make sure she gets the satisfaction of reaching her daily quota.

Be honest, with tact and kindness. Be entirely truthful, but also volunteer information you know your partner wants to know and needs to know. Share your feelings with your partner as well as information and thoughts. And be sure to ask your partner to share his or her feelings with you. When you disagree or argue, talk about the issue without demeaning or blaming your partner. And when you argue or fight, don't clam up. Keep talking until you sort things out.

Opening Lines of Communication

Sit down together and talk through the following questions and any related topics that come up. Write down any questions or issues you wish to discuss further with your counselor.

- *On a scale of one to ten — with one being "poor" and ten being "really great" — how would you rate yourself at fostering intimacy and closeness through your communication with your partner and others?* Why did you rate yourself at this level? Ask your partner how he or she would rate you on this quality and why.

- *How would you rate yourself as an interested, focused, listening communicator?* Why did you rate yourself at his level? Ask your partner how he or she rates you and why.

- *How would you rate yourself on being respectful in communication*? (In other words, free of shaming, blaming, negativity, sarcasm, ridicule, judgments, accusations.) Why this rating? How does your partner rate you and why?

- *How would you rate yourself at being someone who communicates feelings as well as information and thoughts?* Why this rating? How does your partner rate you and why?

6. YOUR FAMILY AFFAIRS:
Understanding family roles and boundaries

A woman caller on *New Life Live* complained to me that her husband talks with his mother on the phone — long conversations — two or three times every single day. It was driving her up the wall because her mother-in-law got more attention from her hubby than she did. Hubby insisted he has always been tight with his mom — and always will be.

It is not unusual for newly married couples to have conflicts over how they will relate to their parents and in-laws after marriage. When you get married, your relationship with your parents changes. Jesus talks about leaving father and mother and being united to each other as the first two members of a new family (see Mark 10:7). Leaving your family of origin doesn't mean they're not your family anymore; it means your new family now takes first importance over your first family.

=== TALK ABOUT IT ===

Understanding Family Roles and Boundaries

Sit down together and talk through the following questions and any related topics that come up. Write down any questions or issues you wish to discuss further with your counselor.

• *How near to your parents and siblings — or far away from — are you comfortable living?* For example, would you take a job if it meant moving across the state from them? A thousand miles away? Across the country? To another continent? Is it your plan to spend your life in the same community as your family? Is it your goal to live within walking distance?

- *How often during the week do you expect to be in contact with family members?* (By phone, text, email, cards and letters, personal visits, etc.)
- *How do you feel about giving family members keys to your house or apartment?*
- *How do you feel about family members dropping in unannounced for a visit?*
- *With whom will you spend the holidays?* (Especially major family gathering times such as Easter, Thanksgiving, and Christmas.) Learn to balance the traditions and expectations of your families of origin with what you and your partner want to establish in your own home.
- *How will you respond to invitations from your family to spend vacations with them?*
- *Under what conditions would you live with your parents and under what conditions would you agree to them moving into your home?*
- *How do you feel about calling your in-laws "Dad and Mom" and having them refer to you as their son or daughter?*
- *How do you feel about expressing your affection to your in-laws with hugs and kisses?*

7. PUT ON A HAPPY FAITH:
Exploring your spiritual life together

Angie grew up in a medium-sized Protestant church where the style of worship was simple and spontaneous. When Angie finished college and moved away to take an inner-city teaching job, she settled into a church similar to her home church.

Then she met Marcus, the man of her dreams in every way — except he was a devout Catholic. As they dated, sometimes Marcus attended Angie's church and sometimes she went to mass with him. Angie was surprised to learn Marcus loved and served God as passionately as she did. She grew to appreciate the beauty, order, and symbolism of Catholic worship. So when Marcus popped the question, she willingly converted and they were married in a Roman Catholic church. Today Angie, Marcus, and their two children are active members of their local parish.

Like Angie and Marcus, it's unlikely your religious upbringing, faith tradition, and spiritual experiences are the same as your partner's, even if you come from a similar church background. So begin dialoguing now about your differences in this area and how you will accommodate them.

=== TALK ABOUT IT ===

Exploring Your Spiritual Life Together

Sit down together and talk through the following questions and any related topics that come up. Write down any questions or issues you wish to discuss further with your counselor.

- *What role does personal faith and religion play in your individual lives?* Now how about in your life as a couple? How large of a role do you want it to play in your life together?

- *What similarities and dissimilarities do you find in your respective faiths, beliefs, and worship styles?*

- *What do you believe is God's purpose for your marriage?* What is his purpose for *you* in your marriage?

- *How do you want to express your faith through your life as a couple? Through your lives individually?*

- *How will you encourage each other's personal faith?* Are you comfortable reading the Bible together and praying together?

- *Once you are married, where will you worship?* Which denomination or church affiliation? Which local church? Which worship style: historic, traditional, contemporary, blended, liturgical and formal, spontaneous and casual, quiet and reverent, joyful and raucous, etc.

- *How frequently will you attend worship services and church-related events such as classes, Bible studies, etc.?* Once a week, twice a week, more often?

- *How will you participate in your church's ministry?* Will you volunteer to teach, sing in the choir, take a leadership role, serve on a committee, etc.?

- *In what faith do you want your children to be raised?*

8. *MONEY MATTERS:*
Accounting for your finance and budget needs

Before meeting Vince, Sasha's finances were an accountant's worst nightmare. She made good money, but she had no budget and kept no receipts. Sasha's method of balancing the checkbook was to close the account and open a new one at another bank. Every year she paid out hundreds of dollars in finance charges, late fees, and overdraft fees. (And you don't even want to know how far behind she was in her taxes!)

Then a cute, starving state tax clerk stepped into her life like an angel of deliverance. Meetings with Vince at the tax office led to dates, and dates opened the door to unofficial financial advice in exchange for Sasha's dynamite *zharkoe* pork and home-baked black bread. She wasn't out of the red by the time they got engaged, but Vince's plan would have her there before they exchanged their vows.

When it comes to personal finances, you and your partner are probably somewhere in the middle ground between Vince and Sasha. But you are about to put your lives — and financial ledgers — together.

TALK ABOUT IT

Accounting for Your Finance and Budget Needs

Sit down together and talk through the following questions and any related topics that come up. Write down any questions or issues you wish to discuss further with your counselor.

- *Are you able to talk about money issues together without getting angry, defensive, or depressed about the subject?* What do you think is behind the emotions you feel over money, budgets, and bills?

- *Which statement better describes you to this point in your life*: "Money is for spending" or "Money is for saving"? How about these two: "Being in debt is normal" or "Being in debt is bad and must be avoided"? Explain your choices.

- *What debts are you bringing into your marriage?* Think about things such as school loans, car payments, a mortgage, credit card debt, and so on. How will you deal with these debts together?

- *What are your long-term financial goals?* In other words, where will your money come from and where do you want it to go? There are good tools out there to help you map out your financial future, including books on financial goals and professionals who specialize in financial planning.

- *Who will make the financial decisions — one of you or both of you?* Is one of you more like Vince: good with numbers, organized, money-savvy, etc.?

- *Who wants to write the checks and take responsibility for paying bills on time?* Is this a once-and-for-always decision or will you take turns paying bills over time?

- *Will you establish and follow a monthly and/or annual budget?* How will you decide how much to spend, save, and give away?

- *Who will take responsibility for organizing and filing financial documents?* (Think bills, receipts, check stubs, statements, tax documents, etc.)

- *Will you have joint bank accounts, separate accounts, or both?*

- *What will be your stance on using credit cards and incurring debt?*

9. *KID ZONE:*
Discussing expectations for children and parenting

"Kids? Get serious, Steve! We're still planning a wedding. We're not ready to talk about kids yet!"

I'm not trying to rush you into starting a family. Take your sweet time. But if you don't talk through your hopes and expectations related to children and parenting now, you may be in for big conflicts and disappointments when you finally address the topic.

TALK ABOUT IT

Discussing Expectations for Children and Parenting

Sit down together and talk through the following questions and any related topics that come up. Write down any questions or issues you wish to discuss further with your counselor.

- *Have you decided if you want to have children some day?* If so, how many and how soon? If not, why not?

- *Are you excited about being parents some day?* What kind of parent do you think will you be?

- *Under what circumstances, if any, would you consider adoption?*

- *Will you use birth control until you're ready for kids?* Have you explored the options for birth control? Have you decided what you will do?

- *Have you decided on your philosophy of parenting and parenting style?* I recommend you find a parenting book both of you generally agree on. Then formulate your philosophy from that book and stick with it. A book helps you devise a good plan instead of parroting or reacting to the way you were raised. It is better to be consistent with a plan that may not be perfect than to be inconsistent without a plan.

- *How do you feel about daycare and babysitting?* Will one of you be a stay-at-home parent?
- *What is your philosophy of child discipline?*
- *Do you favor public school, private school, parochial school, or home school?*
- *Is one of you bringing a child with you into the marriage?* How will you deal with an instant son or daughter? Your first role to a stepchild should be that of a supportive, loving uncle or aunt instead of a controlling, demanding parent. Focus more on loving the child than on correcting or training him or her.
- *How will you communicate your core values and faith to your children?*

10. *THE JOY OF SEX:*
Sharing your sexual needs and fears

You may not be thinking about kids yet, but I'll bet you're thinking about sex! The key is to be talking about sex together as well as thinking about it.

TALK ABOUT IT

Sharing Your Sexual Needs and Fears

Sit down together and talk through the following questions and any related topics that come up. Write down any questions or issues you wish to discuss further with your counselor.

- *How do you feel about talking frankly and openly about sex?* It may be difficult for you, but now is the time to open a lifelong line of communication about your hopes, fears, desires, and needs concerning sex.

- *Where did you get most of your early information about sex?* From parents or other family members, peers, magazines and books, locker room, movies, etc.? How much of what you learned was true and how much was myth or exaggeration?

- *Have you shared, at least in general terms, your past sexual history with each other?* Is it something you want to share and are comfortable sharing?

- *What are your anxieties, worries, or fears as you think about your sex life together?* Here are a number of common concerns about sex couples share:

  - *Sex is evil.* No, sex is good — in fact, it's very good. When he finished creating the universe, which included the creation of

---

200

Adam and Eve and their sex life, God said it was "very good." God created us to enjoy sex within the bounds of marriage. Sex is for procreation and recreation. Your sexual desires for each other are good and right.

– *I'm a novice; I don't know how to do sex.* Perfect sex every time only happens in the movies. Read some wholesome books about sex. Once you're married, you can practice on each other and learn from each other. Laugh about your trials and errors.

– *I don't look or feel very sexy.* No matter how you view yourself, you obviously look sexy to your partner. When it's time for sex, take a shower, apply your favorite fragrance, slip into sexy bedclothes, add soft music and a few candles, then see what happens.

– *My partner and I may not agree on when, where, how, and how often.* Enjoyable sex is about respectfully compromising and selflessly pleasuring each other. Talk about your preferences in these areas and take turns planning the "menu" and being the initiator.

– *I'm afraid someone will hear us or walk in on us.* Part of preparing for sex is making sure you are alone and won't be interrupted. Lock doors, close drapes, and shut off your cell phone. If you have thin apartment walls or guests in another bedroom, have fun practicing "stealth sex" — silent and off the radar.

– *What if my partner isn't in the mood for sex when I am?* A common misconception about sex is that it begins and ends in the bedroom. A popular book by Dr. Kevin Leman helps dispel that myth. It's titled, *Sex Begins in the Kitchen*. What he means by

Sharing Your Sexual Needs and Fears cont.

that title is that satisfying marital sex at bedtime begins with non-sexual caring, tenderness, loving communication, hugs, and handholding throughout the day. What happens under the covers is most satisfying when it is the natural extension of how you love each other in small and special ways all day long.

■

If you think premarital counseling totally prepares you for married life together, you need to go down to the "think" store and stock up. Premarital counseling makes a significant difference in your marriage, but the journey will last a lifetime and you will need to keep learning and growing as you go. I'm adding one more chapter to jumpstart the process once the honeymoon is in your rearview mirror.

10 First-Year Dates after "I Do"

Congratulations! You survived the wedding and you're now "Mr. and Mrs." The wedding cake leftovers are tucked into your grandmother's humongous freezer. Your magical, romantic honeymoon is a dreamy memory. And you two lovebirds go to sleep every night and wake up every morning blessed that the person who vowed to love you for life is lying there next to you feeling just as blessed as you feel. Life couldn't be better, right?

Okay, let's cut the fantasy-land "happily ever after" stuff and get real. Maybe your wedding experience was more like mine. The honeymoon was great, but I wouldn't call it dreamy. And very quickly afterward, the realities of married life came crashing in on me. I had to ask myself the question I am now going to ask you: What happens next?

Answer: You keep on doing the things that got you here. You keep on loving and learning about each other, except now you don't have to go your separate ways at bedtime. You keep on dating, talking, praying, and having fun as you begin the lifetime journey of merging two separate lives into a blended life together. And before you know it you'll be celebrating your first wedding anniversary.

With that in mind, I have one final challenge for you. I want you to go on ten First-Year Counseling Dates to work through ten important marriage growth concepts with each other and then with a professional counselor. The idea is to get the two of you communicating openly about topics that will help your marriage put down healthy first-year roots resulting in a bumper crop of benefits and blessings for the rest of your lives. Talking through these growth concepts with a counselor will further equip you for the transition from being dating singles to a married couple. It will also help you overcome some major barriers most couples encounter. Meeting these issues head on in year one will help lessen any negative impact they may have on your marriage.

As with your premarital counseling, I want you to find an experienced professional counselor with training and experience in the area of marriage counseling. The most logical person to work with you is your premarital counselor, since you already know each other. If he or she is unavailable to you, use the same criteria as before for locating another counselor. Set up a schedule of ten sessions based on the growth concepts covered in this chapter. I suggest you aim at completing these ten sessions over a period of ten to twenty weeks. Use the same plan you followed for the Premarital Counseling Dates by meeting together as a couple for your First-Year Counseling Dates to talk through each topic before you meet with your counselor.

■ 10 Ways to Grow Your Marriage in Year One

You may find it hard to believe, but a lot of married couples tell me their first year of marriage was the hardest. Despite the joy and promise of your life ahead, there are a lot of adjustments to be made. That's why I challenge you to another series of counseling dates on this side of the wedding cake. Like your Premarital Counseling Dates, your First-Year Counseling Dates will help you through the many adjustments of two lives becoming one. Misty and I started our marriage with a series of First-Year Counseling Dates, and we are still enjoying the positive impact of those sessions. I'm confident you will reap the same benefits from your post-marriage First-Year Counseling Dates.

1. HOW CLOSE CAN WE BE?
Making intimacy your top priority

Your top priority for the first year of marriage — and *every* year of your marriage — is to deepen the intimacy of your relationship as husband and wife. It may sound like a tall order, but it really isn't rocket science. You simply learn to do the things that draw you into closer, more intimate connection and avoid doing the things that pull you apart.

I see two ways to nurture intimacy in marriage: deepening your connection and becoming soul mates.

Deepening your connection

Connection is all about constantly moving toward each other, not away from each other. During your first year together you will discover some differences you hadn't noticed before.

For example, you may set the bedside alarm for music, but your partner prefers that toe-curling electronic beep. He sleeps with the bedroom window wide open even if it's thirty degrees; you sleep in a snowsuit and ski mask even in summer. Having differences is okay and totally normal; what is not okay is letting your differences divide you. God willing, you're going to be sleeping next to each other for a lot of years to come. Now is the time to lovingly make room for each other's quirks, needs, and wants. Here are a few keys to deepening your intimate connection with each other.

Talk, talk, talk about everything. Talk about your thoughts, feelings, joys, fears, hopes, disappointments, and so on. Purposely take talk walks and talk timeouts at the coffee shop. Talk before you flip on the TV. Talking doesn't automatically make everything better. But when things are on the surface they can be addressed, understood, and resolved.

Get a graduate degree in your partner's hurts and struggles. You should be so attentive, caring, and compassionate about anything that causes your partner pain that you become the world's number one expert in its prevention and cure without becoming codependent in the process. Come to think of it, a Ph.D. in connecting with each other is even better.

No retreat. If you feel yourself pulling back from your partner emotionally, or feel your partner pulling back from you, move in right away and make connection. Get together for a date, a hand-in-hand walk, or intentionally being in the same room together. Close the physical and emotional space to keep the connection strong.

Get physical. Stay physically close and touchy-feely. I'm not just talking about sex (even though I'm talking about that too).

I'm also talking about frequent touching, hugging, and snuggling non-sexually. Staying physical helps disarm the stress and physical distance that create emotional distance and disconnect. It's called affection, and it's an outward sign of your intimate relationship. It also is the greatest source of and most effective method of foreplay.

Becoming soul mates

The term *"soul mates"* refers to people who are ideally suited to each other. Not many couples are true soul mates when they marry. Rather, most married couples grow to become soul mates over time as connection and intimacy develop between them.

Relationships that are called intimate are close, familiar, warm, private, and personal. Intimacy isn't your marriage's destination; it's the journey that began during dating and courtship and continues through the years and decades of your marriage. This increasingly deeper level of connection between you happens as you work at staying connected at each of the following five areas.

1. *Emotional soul mates.* Emotional intimacy deepens through shared feelings. Pay attention to your own feelings and talk about them with your partner. And stay alert to your partner's feelings and invite him/her to talk about them.

2. *Spiritual soul mates.* Intimacy at the spiritual level grows as you share a spiritual journey together. Spiritual depth is encouraged as you pray and study the Bible together, attend church and Bible studies together, serve God

together, talk about your spiritual doubts, and share openly what you hear God saying to you.

3. *Intellectual soul mates.* Shared insight and understanding fosters intellectual intimacy. This happens as you discuss what you read and think about such things as current events, politics, world view, and the economy. You also grow together in this area as you set, pursue, and evaluate personal and marriage goals together.

4. *Sexual soul mates.* If you think sex is fun now just wait a few years. Closeness in sex deepens over time as you pursue together a mutually satisfying sexual experience. Sexual intimacy feeds off of open dialog — talking about how the two of you want to "do sex," as in how often, where, when, and how.

5. *Friendship soul mates.* Intimacy deepens as you become closer friends through shared activities such as hobbies, sports, dates, games, and just having fun. Make plenty of room in your day-to-day lives for things that bring grins, giggles, and belly laughs.

Making Intimacy Your Top Priority

Sit down together and talk through the following questions and any related topics that come up. Write down any questions or issues you wish to discuss further with your counselor.

- *When do you feel the greatest emotional connection to each other?* At what times or in what settings do you feel less connected?

- **When do you do your best talking about your lives and relationship?** What kinds of things tend to prevent or interrupt these times together? What can you do individually and as a couple to make sure you have time to connect conversationally?

- *How skilled are you at perceiving and alleviating your partner's hurts and struggles and how skilled is your partner in comforting you in your areas of pain?* How could your partner best help you earn that advanced degree in his/her difficulties?

- *What does your partner need to know about how his or her touch helps or hinders connection with you?*

- *Think about one or two married couples you know who seem to be true soul mates: What do you see in them that fits the description of soul mates?*

- *Consider your progress:* In which of the five areas of intimacy presented above would you say, "I think we're well on our way to becoming soul mates"? In which areas would you say, "We have some growing to do in this area"?

- *What are some ways you will pursue intimacy in each of the five areas?*

2. *DO YOU ALWAYS GET WHAT YOU WANT? (ME NEITHER!):* Confronting feelings of entitlement

This issue undoubtedly came up during your days of dating and courtship and I'm hoping you dealt with it. Now that you're married, you need to address it again. You must find out what each of you feels entitled to and how each of you feels about what your partner feels entitled to. He might feel entitled to watch sports on Sunday from as soon as you get home from church until bedtime. Are you going to let him have his way? She may feel entitled to be out with the girls one night every week. Is that okay with you?

One of the most common areas where couples clash over entitlement is personal space, and it can cause problems, For example, Maggie and Joel had been married about four months when a surprising thought caught Joel off guard: *Maggie is never, ever going home. She lives with me twenty-four-seven.* The thought happened one day when he was heading for his comfy old leather recliner to do some reading. When he got there he found it piled high with Maggie's laundry fresh from the dryer. Joel never had to share his chair with laundry before he got married. He saw that pile of clothes as an invasion of his personal space.

As much as married people enjoy sharing time and space together, I haven't met any who don't also value time alone occasionally and a little space — such as Joel's old chair — they can call their own. Most marriage experts say it's healthy to balance a couple's together time with personal time for each partner. When each of you are able to get off by yourself to read or relax or do something else you enjoy, it helps keep your together time fresh.

We're talking about a couple things here: personal space in your schedule and personal space in your environment. Everybody can use a little me-time now and then to think, pray, create, work out, meditate, snooze, work, play a game, watch a favorite TV show, or whatever. It's even better when you have a little corner of the world that is your space for doing what you want to do — scrapbooking room, man cave, corner of the living room for an "office," puttering room, attic, a gazebo in the yard, or simply "my chair."

Maybe me-time and space for you means getting out with other people: a Bible study or accountability group, a poker night or ball game with the guys, a chick flick or shopping with the girlfriends, and so on. Pursuing some of your own interests apart from your partner helps build intimacy in your relationship. It gives you something else to talk about — where you went, what you did, who you saw, etc.

When carving out personal space for yourself and your partner, keep a few guidelines in mind:

Book your dates. Put your me-time activities on the calendar when it works for both you and your partner. Help each other keep those dates clear for getting away.

Get spaced out. Work together to identify "your space" and "my space" where you live. Then honor each other's space by not cluttering it with your stuff or demanding that it meet your standards for decoration or neatness.

Guard the borders. When it's your time in your space, don't let false guilt rob you of the time out you need.

Be thankful. Thank your partner for honoring your need for time and space apart.

Confronting Feelings of Entitlement

Sit down together and talk through the following questions and any related topics that come up. Write down any questions or issues you wish to discuss further with your counselor.

- *In light of your relationship with your partner, how would you describe your need and/or desire for time alone and personal space?* How do you feel taking time for yourself?

- *If you had an afternoon or evening to do whatever you wanted to do without your partner, what are some things that would be on your list?* How about a day alone? A weekend?

- *What kind of personal space at home and/or away from home would you consider ideal for doing what you like to do?* What would it take to prepare that space for your use?

- *What boundaries would you place on your personal time and personal space?* What input would you like to give your partner on his or her personal time and personal space?

3. *I SURE DIDN'T EXPECT THAT:*
Getting over disappointments in marriage

Even if you've only been married a few hours, days, or weeks, I'm sure you know what I mean by marriage disappointments. There have already been things in your relationship that didn't quite meet your expectations and hopes. Well, you'd better get used to it because the words *"perfect"* and *"marriage"* hardly ever show up in the same sentence. For example, here are a number of possible clues married life won't always live up to your standards:

- She didn't know he wore platform shoes until he took them off on the honeymoon and the two of them were no longer seeing eye to eye.

- Your partner announces he or she never learned how to use an iron and doesn't intend to now. (That's right, if you can't wear it right out of the dryer, you're on your own.)

- Your attempt to establish a new world record by having sex every single night of your marriage has already been thwarted (several times, in fact).

- If the screwdriver didn't have a big red handle, the handyman you thought you married wouldn't know which end to use.

Disappointments in all marriages are a given. You just have to decide what the two of you will do with them. Is it appropriate to express your disappointments to your partner? And if so, how do you say it?

Here's my take on those key points. I believe it's important to verbalize your disappointments to each other in a positive, caring way because it's the only way to change things that can be changed and find peace when disappointing things cannot be changed. If you try to suppress feelings of disappointment, it won't work. Your hurt will eventually boil out of you in anger or criticism, and that's bad news for a good marriage. And if you don't feel comfortable or safe expressing your disappointments to each other, talking about it openly can create new levels of understanding and connection between you.

A lot of disappointments can be "fixed," meaning they are derived from behaviors that can be changed. For example, if it really bugs you that your partner throws dirty clothes and towels on the floor, expressing your disappointment in a non-accusing way may open the door for him or her to change. Problem solved!

Other disappointments can't be fixed, so you learn to "peacefully coexist" in spite of them. If your partner is not the handy-person type, it's okay to call a fix-it person when the drain plugs up. And so what if your partner's singing in the shower sounds like a cat that just got stepped on? Just be happy your dear one isn't crying in the shower because you can't get over living with a monotone.

Getting Over Disappointment in Marriage

Sit down together and talk through the following questions and any related topics that come up. Write down any questions or issues you wish to discuss further with your counselor.

- *How do you feel about expressing your marriage disappointments to your partner?* Where do you think these feelings come from?

- *What are some disappointments in your marriage that can possibly be fixed?* Express them to each other in a positive way, not with demands, threats, or ultimatums.

- *What are some disappointments in your marriage that cannot be fixed?* How will you work around these immoveable objects to benefit your relationship?

4. *JUST THE WAY YOU ARE:*
Accepting each other unconditionally and demonstrating your appreciation

While they were dating, Liz didn't complain to Raul about his "socially-challenged" shyness. Her guy was the catch of a lifetime in every other way, so she accommodated his quiet (and to her, boring) lifestyle.

After the wedding, it was a different story. Liz felt it was her duty to give Raul a social makeover. She invited people to their apartment every weekend — friends, neighbors, family, even strangers. And when he asked her to lighten up a little on the social calendar, she chided, "Baby, you need me to help you get in touch with your party side." Liz was shocked one Friday night when Raul jumped into his car and left for the evening without a word, just as her guests were arriving.

I've heard a lot of stories like this from newly married couples. One or both partners are very accepting during courtship, trying to make the best impression. Then they use the marriage license as a construction permit to whip their partner into shape and grind off the rough edges. Quirks or behavior traits they might overlook in someone else are seen as fair game in a husband or wife.

Every one of us has a powerful need to be accepted just as we are, faults and all. When we know we are accepted by others we feel significant, wanted, valuable, and loved. Lack of acceptance makes us feel unimportant, unwanted, and useless. Accepting someone without strings doesn't mean you're blind to their weaknesses or failures. It simply means you choose not to hold their weaknesses and failures against them. Instead of pointing out faults, acceptance persistently points out strengths.

It's vital to the long-term health and happiness of your marriage that you accept your partner "as is" instead of trying to change him or her. Acceptance is the evidence of unconditional love, the kind of love that takes people as they are without demanding something in return. There is much greater potential for your partner to change if you accept him or her.

One of the most important ways to demonstrate your acceptance is to express your appreciation for your partner by communicating the ways he or she makes you feel good. For example:

"You filled up my car's tank — how sweet!"

"I'm so happy being married to you."

"Thanks for taking out the garbage."

"That outfit blows me away. You look great!"

"I love it when you make me laugh."

"You rock my world, babe!"

Nonverbal appreciation can be just as powerful. You can tell your partner "thanks" and "I love you" through your time and attention and acts of affection, courtesy, and pampering.

One of the deadly pitfalls in marriage is taking your partner and what he or she does for you for granted. Find something you appreciate about your partner every day and let him or her know about it: a note on the pillow, a text, a little gift, a kiss and a squeeze, a whisper, a voicemail, or some other creative expression. Appreciation is valued all the time but it is especially needed if your partner is having a real crummy day. And when you are generous with your appreciation, your partner will be generous at continuing to make you feel good!

If you ever run short of things to appreciate in your partner, think about what he or she may have given up to get married (including not having to put up with you). Also, imagine what your partner's daily life is like hour by hour — activities, responsibilities, difficulties. What do you appreciate about all that he or she does through the day? Now communicate it.

Accepting Each Other Unconditionally and Demonstrating Your Appreciation

Sit down together and talk through the following questions and any related topics that come up. Write down any questions or issues you wish to discuss further with your counselor.

- *List several strengths and positive qualities you admire in your partner.*

- *How does your partner demonstrate he or she accepts you unconditionally despite your flaws?* How do you try to demonstrate your acceptance?

- *How do you feel when your partner affirms your strengths and successes while minimizing your weaknesses and mistakes?*

- *What changes would you like to make in your life that could improve the harmony of your relationship?*

- *What do you most appreciate about your partner?* Put together a thoughtful list of his or her most endearing qualities, traits, and actions. Then share your lists with each other.

- *How do you feel hearing your partner express appreciation for you?* How does it make you want to respond?

5. *WHEN THE ANSWER IS ALWAYS NO:*
Overcoming stubborn resistance

Your partner wants the both of you to attend a couples Sunday school class at church, but you've dug in your heels. The Sunday morning worship service is all you're ready to do. You've been bugging your partner to get an annual physical, but all you get from him or her is, "I'm not going to the doc unless I'm sick, and I'm never sick."

If the issue of stubborn resistance has already raised its ugly head in your relationship, deal with it and the feelings behind it now. Ask your counselor to explain what it means to be truly willing to accommodate your partner, for your willingness in large part determines the depth of your life together.

TALK ABOUT IT

Overcoming Stubborn Resistance

Sit down together and talk through the following questions and any related topics that come up. Write down any questions or issues you wish to discuss further with your counselor.

- *In what areas are you resisting something your partner wants from you or for you?* In what areas is he/she resisting you?

- *How do you feel about the stalemate in these areas?*

- *What would it take for you to relent in areas where you're now resisting?*

---

6. WHEN YOU DON'T AGREE:
Thriving through conflict

After my many years of training and experience as a marriage therapist, I have finally come up with the recipe for a perfect marriage. All you have to do is find a man and a woman who are perfectly compatible with each other and let them get married. That's right; I'm pulling your leg. There's no such thing as a perfectly compatible couple. And that includes the two of you, even though right now you may think you're pretty darn close.

Your marriage, like everyone else's, is made up of two imperfect people with different histories, personalities, quirks, weaknesses, interests, and needs. Even in the most loving marriages these differences will occasionally erupt into conflicts of opinion and action. It's not a matter of *if* you will have conflict; it's a matter of when and how you respond. Here are some positive ways to resolve conflict and bless and strengthen your marriage:

Fight for love. "Resolving conflict" doesn't mean doing whatever you can to win the argument. It means doing whatever you can to deepen your love for each other in the midst of a difficulty.

Honor some rules of engagement. Whenever you clash over something, set up a time when the two of you can talk it through without distractions. Take turns calmly expressing your feelings, fears, and hurts. Focus on each other and listen to each other without interrupting.

Own up to your part. Don't duck your guilt in the matter. Admit your mistakes honestly without trying to shift the blame to your partner. When you're at fault, apologize and ask your partner to forgive you. When your partner is wrong, accept his or her apology graciously and forgive him or her.

Fight fairly. No low blows, such as having angry tirades, name-calling, dredging up past offenses, abusing verbally or physically, or bad-mouthing your partner in front of others. If you sense you're losing control, take time out to cool down.

Hang in there for closure. Don't let emotions or interruptions keep you from resolving the issue. Keep at it until peace is restored.

=== TALK ABOUT IT ===

Thriving through Conflict

Sit down together and talk through the following questions and any related topics that come up. Write down any questions or issues you wish to discuss further with your counselor.

- *What general areas of conflict have already surfaced in your relationship?*

- *What has been your pattern for dealing with your conflicts?* How has that pattern worked for you?

- *Have you experienced any conflicts that have not been resolved?* Why do you think they have resisted resolution?

- *Which of the conflict resolution tips above do you think will be the most helpful to your growth in resolving conflict?*

7. I'M SORRY, I WAS WRONG:
Expressing and healing justifiable resentment through forgiveness

There will be times when your partner wrongs you and you will boil with resentment for good reason. When it happens you can either cling to and nurture your resentment or you can begin the tough process of healing through forgiveness.

Nothing can do more to promote health and longevity in your marriage than forgiveness. You will both have bad days and screw up. As much as you love each other, you will do things and say things that prompt misunderstanding, anger, hurt, and tears in your partner. You'll occasionally do the wrong thing or not do the right thing. And you will both be guilty at times, that's for sure, so you both need to forgive and be forgiven. And even when you're not aware of any hurts you may have caused, it's a good idea to take time out to preemptively say, "Are we okay? Is there anything between us we need to clear up?"

Here are several important things you need to know about forgiveness:

It's a decision. Don't wait until you feel like forgiving your partner. Choose to forgive even when you're heartbroken or spitting mad. Your feelings will catch up to your decision eventually.

It's an antidote. Forgiveness stops the hurt and pain of an offense and restores health. It clears the deck of offenses so you can move forward. Withholding forgiveness opens the door to deeper hurt and bitterness.

It's an act of grace. Forgiveness doesn't mean your partner didn't hurt you. Your forgiveness may not be deserved, but you forgive anyway. It's your opportunity to demonstrate how deeply you love your partner.

It's free. Forgiveness doesn't say, "I'll forgive you if ..." Or "You owe me big time for this." No revenge, no retribution, no emotional blackmail. If you make your partner pay for it, work for it, or suck up for it, it isn't true forgiveness.

It's over. Once you forgive, let it go and let your partner off the hook. Don't ever use the offense against him or her.

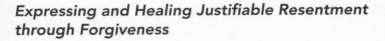

TALK ABOUT IT

Expressing and Healing Justifiable Resentment through Forgiveness

Sit down together and talk through the following questions and any related topics that come up. Write down any questions or issues you wish to discuss further with your counselor.

- *How difficult is it for you to forgive the wrongs of others?* How difficult is it for you to ask forgiveness from those you wrong?

- *Can you think of any ways I have offended you and failed to ask your forgiveness?* Take turns asking and responding to that question.

8. THE WAY TO UP IS DOWN:
Taking the low road of humility

Do you remember the character Westley, played by Cary Elwes, in the classic family movie *The Princess Bride*? He's the farmhand in love with his mistress, Buttercup (Robin Wright), who regards him as nothing more than a servant. But Westley wins his love's heart with selfless, devoted service. No matter what she asks him to do, Westley does it, saying with deference and courtesy, "As you wish." And when Buttercup falls into the clutches of the evil prince, Westley cheats death at every turn to save his true love. What a guy!

Westley is a great picture of what humility can look like in relationships. Humility takes the low road of honoring and serving others instead of expecting or demanding to be honored and served. Here are a few ideas for how the "As you wish" attitude could play out in your marriage:

- *Consider it a mission from God.* View yourself as God's instrument to bless and serve your partner, especially in the little, day-by-day things.

- *Look for times to say "After you."* Put your partner's needs and wants before your own, not when you feel like it but whenever you see the opportunity.

- *Be a hero.* Work just as hard to relieve your partner's pain and stress as you would your own.

- *Give credit abundantly when due.* Graciously acknowledge and receive your partner's effort, ideas, and contributions.

- *Go ahead and say, "My bad."* Admit your mistakes instead of trying to justify them. And when your partner is wrong and apologizes, be gracious.

- *Make someone happy.* Make it your aim to do whatever makes your partner happy and avoid anything that makes him or her unhappy, even if it makes you unhappy.

A word of warning: Don't get into a big fight trying to decide who will serve whom. There's opportunity for mutually give and take in your expressions of humility. For example, some mornings you will get up first to make coffee for your partner. But when your partner beats you out of bed and makes coffee for you, enjoy and be thankful. Make it a friendly competition of serving each other in as many ways as possible.

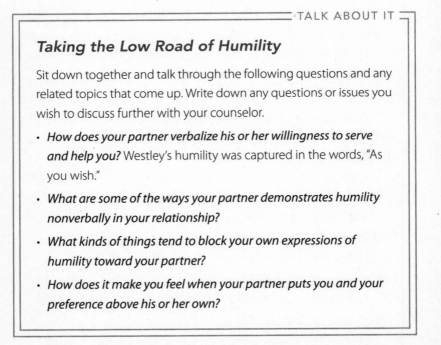

TALK ABOUT IT

Taking the Low Road of Humility

Sit down together and talk through the following questions and any related topics that come up. Write down any questions or issues you wish to discuss further with your counselor.

- *How does your partner verbalize his or her willingness to serve and help you?* Westley's humility was captured in the words, "As you wish."

- *What are some of the ways your partner demonstrates humility nonverbally in your relationship?*

- *What kinds of things tend to block your own expressions of humility toward your partner?*

- *How does it make you feel when your partner puts you and your preference above his or her own?*

9. GET REAL WITH YOUR EXPECTATIONS:
Loving your partner when it's tough

The Ten-Date Challenge is all about getting to know your partner at a deep level through extensive, purposeful dating before you marry. The reasoning is simple: The more you learn about each other on the pre-marriage side of the wedding cake, the fewer unpleasant surprises and marriage-rocking regrets you'll experience after the ceremony.

But there are no guarantees, because it's impossible to know everything about each other before you say "I do." Furthermore, you don't know how the future will impact your individual lives and your marriage. That's why traditional marriage vows include the vow of commitment through sickness and health, poverty and wealth, and so on. What happens when one of you is diagnosed with cancer or mental illness or is permanently disabled in an accident? In other words, what do you do when the person you married is unable to fulfill your expectations and sense of entitlement due to unforeseen changes lurking ahead?

There is only one process that works for this: *You lower your expectations and accept the reality of your relationship.* And you do it every day if you want a long-lasting vibrant relationship.

Loving Your Partner When It's Tough

Sit down together and talk through the following questions and any related topics that come up. Write down any questions or issues you wish to discuss further with your counselor.

- *How do you feel about the prospect that your partner may for some reason be unable to fulfill your expectations in the marriage relationship?* How do you feel about being unable to fulfill your partner's expectations due to something beyond your control?
- *Have unfulfilled expectations surfaced in your marriage so far?* If so, what are they? How have they impacted your relationship?

10. *DIFFERENT STROKES:*
Sharing like values and blending the rest

If you were smart, you married someone who shares most if not all of your core values. But sometimes that kind of smarts doesn't come into play until after the wedding. If you find yourself butting heads over values such as faith and religion, worldviews, politics, etc., ask your counselor to help you explore the values you do share and build on those to bring unity and direction in your relationship. And be willing to make some compromises. For example, you may be a fundamentalist Protestant who married a staunch Roman Catholic. You have to ask yourself how you two ever got together. But then you have to find a way to turn the potential conflict of your differences into a major strength in your marriage and other marriages you share your journey with.

Sharing Like Values and Blending the Rest

Sit down together and talk through the following questions and any related topics that come up. Write down any questions or issues you wish to discuss further with your counselor.

- *Which statement best describes you as a couple?* (1) We dated and married largely because we share similar values; (2) Values were not a huge factor in bringing us together, but we did have a couple of important non-negotiables; (3) We dated and married without much concern that we may have widely different values.

- *Where are your values most compatible?* Where are they least compatible? How have you handled any areas where your values conflict?

■

As you apply these ten growth principles to your relationship this year and in the years to come, you will be able to describe your marriage in many ways. But one of the words that should never describe your marriage is *"boring."* If your marriage gets boring it means you've stopped growing together, connecting, and deepening intimacy. So don't let your post-marriage growth dates ever come to an end. You have a lifetime together ahead of you. Use every year of that lifetime to grow as closely together as you can and enjoy the fun and fulfillment that comes from that commitment.

I'm so happy you care enough about your life together to

invest the time and expense for dealing with these growth issues. I assure you that you will recoup that investment many times over as your love deepens and as the two of you bless each other and everyone around you.

So Are You Ready to Say "I Do"?

If you are ready to say "I do," I wanted to leave you with a couple of pointers that might help. They sure helped me. Just in case you are wondering, my wife and I have been an item for eight years, and I can tell you in all honesty, no author distortion or literary liberties taken, that we are having the most connected, most fun and fulfilling marriage I know possible. In my mind there is no one on the planet who would be better to be married to. What is exciting to me is that it gets better and better and we grow closer and closer. So it is possible to mess up and then, maybe for the first time, make a very good choice. But you have to take your time.

Everything I presented here went into our dating. All of the timing guidelines and counseling and fun suggestions were part of our dating. By the time we were married we knew each other well enough to know it would not be easy at first, but once we got in sync, it could be an amazing marriage. And that is what it has turned out to be.

If she or I had been looking for perfection or had unrealistic expectations, we would have never pulled out of that first year of struggle and gotten on with a marriage that is strong and secure. So from personal experience I can tell you that while these efforts at ten dates may seem troublesome and even annoying, they produce long-term, lasting results. At least they have for us. But they don't prevent conflict and struggle.

Marriage is always an adjustment, even for the most perfect couple (whatever that is). We struggled to adjust, but we struggled forward. Divorce was never an option at the worst point of our first year, so we either had to get better or we would be stuck in adjustment, turmoil, and conflict. My point here is, be ready for some tough times. Be prepared to think you married the wrong person and made a huge mistake. Just keep moving forward and it will soon pass.

So as you launch out or relaunch, be realistic in your expectations. A crummy first year of marriage is not a prognosis. Determine that the one thing you bring into the relationship is a persevering attitude. And hopefully the *Is This The One?* material will greatly reduce your perseverance time and increase your Above and Beyond Expectation time.

I have loved writing this book, thinking of someone just like you who just like me would be willing to take this dating challenge. My prayer for you is that your marriage be a blessing to you and those who know you.

If you have any questions or comments, I can be reached at SArterburn@newlife.com

America's #1 Christian Counseling Call-in Show

New Life Live
WITH STEVE ARTERBURN
CONNECTION   TRUTH   TRANSFORMATION

With your host
Steve Arterburn
"See you on the radio..."

New Life Live Co-Hosts:

Dr. Jill Hubbard Dr. Dave Stoop Dr. Henry Cloud Dr. John Townsend Dr. Sheri Denham Rev. Milan Yerkovich

New Life Live is unique in that the host and co-hosts offer the truth straight up, but they do so with a mix of candor, compassion and humor that is unmatched. They help callers see and deal with reality in a loving and non-judgmental manner. The result is a following that brings new and loyal listeners to radio and TV stations across the country.

Listen to *New Life Live* on XM or Sirius satellite radio, channel 131, Family Talk at 1:00pm Eastern.
Call 1-800-NEW-LIFE (639-5433) or go to newlife.com to find a local station near you and the time it airs.
Or listen online at newlife.com.

The show is broadcast on television and can be found on FamilyNet or NRB networks.

TRANSFORMATION
It starts with a weekend workshop

New Life Weekend

For those who struggle with fear, anger, depression, abuse, marriage, grief, self-worth, forgiveness, boundaries or related issues.

"I came with my hopes kept in check. Boy was I wrong! I am amazed at the huge work God did in just 2 days. I feel cleansed, refreshed, recharged and free to take the next "best step" for me. My anxiety has been replaced with excitement." —Donna

Marriage—Through It All, Better Than Ever

No one does marriage weekends like we do. Whether you are looking for a tune-up or your marriage is in need of rescue—this weekend is for you. The results will be a restored and renewed marriage.

"We were in a 20 year mess...we were so stuck! This weekend has been full of hope and fun! I leave here with real hope, a deeper connection with my God, new friends and tools to help my marriage not just survive, but "thrive!" —Lynn

Lose It for Life

Discover the total solution for permanent weight loss. It's not about what you eat, it's about what's eating you. We can help you deal with your "it" once and for all.

"I was absolutely miserable with my body, my life. This event has been life-changing! I leave here with a new awareness, a new self-worth, with things surrendered, and a new plan!" —Heidi

All workshops include small groups led by licensed Christian Counselors

1-800-NEW-LIFE   newlife.com